16.

This is Today …

This is Today ...

A BIOGRAPHY OF THE TODAY PROGRAMME

TIM LUCKHURST

Aurum Press

First published in Great Britain
2001 by Aurum Press Ltd
25 Bedford Avenue, London WC1B 3AT

Copyright © 2001 Tim Luckhurst

Design by Geoff Green at Geoff Green Book Design

A catalogue record for this book is available from the British Library.

Lines from 'No Entry' on p.xi © Andrew Motion 2001 reprinted by permission of PFD
on behalf of Andrew Motion.

ISBN 1 85410 797 6

1 3 5 7 9 10 8 6 4 2
2001 2003 2005 2004 2002

Printed in Great Britain
by MPG Books Ltd, Bodmin

This book is dedicated to Dorothy, Phoebe, Toby, Georgia and Molly, my late brother Dr Matthew Luckhurst, my sister Dr Heidi Luckhurst and my parents.

Contents

Introduction   ix

ONE   The Early Years of *Today*   1
TWO   *Today*'s Golden Years   17
THREE The Best Job in Journalism   35
FOUR   The Magic of Radio   54
FIVE   Who Listens to *Today*?   73
SIX   The Things They Do for *Today*   95
SEVEN 'Thought for the Day'   117
EIGHT *Today* and Spin   135
NINE   *Today*'s Dilemma   152

Acknowledgements   175

Introduction

E litist, genteel and old-fashioned as its many critics think it, the *Today* programme is probably the nearest thing to a collective sense of identity the modern British middle class still possesses. Only a small minority attends church. Active participation in party politics is going the same way as religious observance. Communication, even with friends, is as likely to take place via e-mail as by face to face conversation.

Today is a rare element of shared experience in an increasingly fragmented world. It is the virtual reality in which 6 million concerned and responsible citizens hear about the issues that matter to them. They do not agree about the solutions but they reach consensus about the agenda. Generations that once learned from the same textbooks or rushed into work to repeat the same jokes have found a new bond, something of a plurality of experience. The programme offers a badge of membership, a sense of belonging.

Precise definition of a phenomenon so widely shared and appreciated is difficult. The *Today* team certainly think so. 'We who present and produce it are very proud of *Today*,' explained one of its most distinguished presenters, John Humphrys, on the programme's fortieth birthday in 1997, 'but ask us exactly what it is and we have a bit of a problem. It's not just news, even though everyone says we set the agenda and our most important task is to keep you informed. We also want to keep you entertained. If we bore you, we lose you.' Then he paraphrased one of his predecessors, the late Brian Redhead, who had defined *Today* as 'a great many powerful, interesting, funny, angry, brave, frightened people dropping a word in the ear of the nation'. Humphrys concluded with his own stab at categorization: for him the programme was 'a ringside seat at history'.

Today is all of these things. It is a compendium of interviews, events and controversies that amounts to more than the sum of its parts. It is a powerful tool in British political debate and a window on the wider world. Somehow, the whole has become an expression of identity that comes closer than anything else to defining what it means to be a concerned and active British citizen in a complex and diverse world.

30 March 2001. Britain, or that part of Britain which cares about such things, waited with growing irritation for the Prime Minister to make up his mind. Would the burgeoning crisis of foot and mouth disease, spreading through the country's livestock herds for the first time since the 1960s, postpone the general election long planned for 3 May? Could Tony Blair be persuaded to abandon his meticulously prepared campaign timetable in deference to the suffering of farmers and hoteliers?

Today asked the question directly in a discussion between the Prime Minister's former adviser, Tim Allan, and the veteran psephologist Bob Worcester. Allan explained that Blair's choice would be a lonely one. Different members of his advisory team would offer coherent arguments for and against the anticipated date. In the end the Prime Minister would have to make his own choice in the face of conflicting opinion.

It wasn't supposed to be like that. Foot and mouth had crept up on the government, spreading ever further across the country as ministers, first blithely and then with obvious nervousness, insisted the disease was 'under control'. By that morning everyone knew it wasn't. General Sir Michael Jackson, the soldier who had led British troops during the liberation of Kosovo, was reduced to providing logistical support for the slaughter and burial of sheep. *Today* had noted the changing mood, from foot and mouth being regarded as a bizarre reminder of a forgotten pattern of life, to a new awareness that the virus was making Britain look medieval and filthy. Tony Blair's 'New Britain' is meant to look modern and dynamic, never filthy.

The programme captured the zeitgeist with an impressive exclusive. At 8.20 a.m. the Poet Laureate, Andrew Motion, appeared on the show to read his new poem about foot and mouth. Called simply 'No Entry', it began:

Where the lane curved, and sidled sideways as if tricked by a water-burst,
and the fawn gravel dwindled into clay
thinning above a fabulous patchwork
of pressed car bodies buried to make a path,
there was this dense, ivy decked thorn hedge

I could see over and into the square
Red Tabor had made home for his one sow –
slumped, a massive, fierce but dingy orange
pineapple skin, embarrassing nude quivers
under a hail of flies – snoozing and snorting
her slow days through between litters.

What better way to capture the significance of the crisis and the
sentiments of the nation beyond Whitehall? The Poet Laureate,
performing his role amidst the 'drizzling screen / of long fires
and longer trench-gashes, timber and tyre smoke-castles'.
Motion evoked 'their black barbecue stench / impossible to catch
but not to remember' which filled the countryside.

But he did not deliver his words to the Queen or read from
the pulpit at Westminster Abbey. Motion's poetry spoke directly
to and for the concerned citizens of Britain. He judged, rightly,
that publication on *Today* would reach that constituency. For
hours afterwards, the *Today* programme website, on which the
text of his specially commissioned poem was displayed, was
jammed by listeners seeking access. The Prime Minister, meanwhile, postponed the election.

Something similar had happened a few weeks earlier. *Today*
broadcast a discussion about the new method of assessing social
class that was to be used to compile the national census. The programme then posted a 'check your class' questionnaire on its
website; 100,000 people rushed to assess their status.

Using the rapier of poetry to replace the cudgel of political
argument, or the instant judgement of the internet to replace
hours of agonized debate over accent, income and old school tie,
are perfect examples of the way *Today* has finessed its role in
British life. The programme has learned to take the temperature
of the thinking nation, to read its mood and then broadcast the
findings back to the people they emerged from in a way which
tells them more than they originally knew about themselves.

As the world has become complicated for Britain's agenda-setting news and current affairs programme, so this instinctive approach is increasingly important. For years as the Conservative Party eviscerated itself in public, *Today* needed to do little more in order to inform and entertain than invite MPs and ministers to air their grievances. Many seemed to regard it as their constitutional duty. From the mid-1980s until the 1997 general election, politics often took place on *Today*. As the real cockpit of national debate, it was a more entertaining forum than the House of Commons. Direct questions were asked, language was informal, evasion was not tolerated. Ministers used it to launch policy initiatives. *Today* staff remember the occasion when Kenneth Clarke, then Education Secretary in Mrs Thatcher's Cabinet, arrived to discuss an initiative concerning schools, unaware that the Chancellor of the Exchequer, Nigel Lawson, had offered a substantial new spending allocation to his department. Clarke heard about the new money for the first time in the news bulletin that preceded his interview. He pretended to be fully briefed, then emerged from the studio to admit to a *Today* producer that the first he'd heard of Nigel's spending plans was in the programme's news bulletin – 'I nearly drove into the ditch on my way in.'

That kind of thing still happens, but *Today* has to work harder to get it and, crucially, political affiliation has ceased to be the primary indicator of class or attitude. The wealthy are as likely to vote Labour as they are to support the Tories. Identity has become a more disparate phenomenon. Ministers in the acutely media-savvy Labour government believe in controlling the news, not contributing to it. They bully, cajole and threaten broadcasters. Voters in turn have become acutely sceptical about the political process. They care about politics but do not easily trust politicians.

Today has been forced to think laterally in order to survive. The programme has rediscovered the importance of entertaining listeners as well as informing them, and of broadcasting their concerns to the leaders elected to serve them, not just presenting the arguments of politicians for assessment by the public. Now, controversial opinion is as likely to emerge in the form of essays by maverick commentators such as the novelists Will Self and

Frederick Forsyth as in a straight confrontation between John Humphrys and a minister. Humour, style and investigative reporting have taken their place alongside set-piece interviews. A modern form of the humanity once injected by Brian Redhead, Jack de Manio, Peter Hobday and John Timpson has crept back into the programme.

Today still sets Britain's agenda, but, increasingly, it does that by being accessible and sometimes deliberately controversial. The modern *Today* programme believes it has a duty to broadcast opinions which challenge the status quo in the political arena and beyond. It has rediscovered a passion for literature, film, music and the environment. It employs dedicated specialist reporters to ferret out news the establishment does not want to hear discussed. Adversity has given the programme new confidence. It has made *Today* more aware of its real audience, the 6 million ordinary Britons who are neither politicians nor spin doctors but who wake up to *Today* and regard it as a trusted part of their daily routine.

If the *Today* programme was able to get away with being 'Westminster Village Radio' during the years of Tory meltdown, it has had to be more broad-minded since. The presenters can still grill a cornered politician quickly over a high flame, but *Today* has hinterland too. It explores the wildlife present in British gardens, debates the nature and meaning of social class, provides a home for fine writing and unmediated opinion.

Today has returned to the instincts that first made it popular. After a period of political obsession, new competition and a seriously diminished audience, it has found a way to make old principles work in a new environment. Competition from twenty-four hour radio news channels and a plethora of specialist services on digital and satellite television has been confronted and defeated. *Today*'s audience, which dipped alarmingly between 1997 and 1998, has returned to the familiar voices of John Humphrys, Sue MacGregor and Jim Naughtie and the increasingly familiar ones of a group of new contenders. As bacon and egg was once consumed to the sound of Jack de Manio and toast eaten in the company of Brian Redhead, so a new generation of listeners now shower, shave, wash children and hasten to work to the rhythm of *Today*. One British institution has achieved the Blairite dream of asserting old principles in a new context.

In February 2001 the BBC contracted Allan Little to present *Today* for a minimum of sixty days per year. After years abroad as the BBC's man in South Africa, Moscow, Sarajevo and Baghdad and an apprenticeship as a *Today* reporter, Little returned to Britain to be the new boy on the team. He is starting out where John Humphrys started fourteen years ago, a foreign correspondent coming home to take a place at the heart of the nation's affairs. Little has taken time to think about what *Today* means. 'It's a national conversation – and Britain is still a very important country, with a global perspective. So *Today* is about an important country having an important conversation about itself. And that happens on the *Today* programme more effectively than it happens anywhere else in Britain or the world. I've never heard anything else like it.'

Britain's Chief Rabbi, the author and philosopher Dr Jonathan Sacks, who regularly contributes to the programme's 'Thought for the Day' slot, adds that he has 'personal experience of cases where a major national decision was taken on the basis of comments made on the *Today* programme'. For him, *Today* is unique, an essential part of modern Britain, important enough to include elements which are 'wacky, eccentric and wholly benign… like everything else that's great in British culture'.

That, in any event, is the case for the defence.

But there are, of course, many who regard such praise as absurd. To the enormous constituency of Britons who do not listen and never will, *Today* is synonymous with Oxbridge, public schools, snobbery and disdain. One critic describes the programme as 'so far up its own arse it's drowning in something unpleasant'. To such commentators, *Today* is merely a relic of the old BBC home service, a geriatric throwback to the days of the Empire. But perhaps such hostility is provoked more by the programme's refusal to oversimplify, or treat *EastEnders* as the cultural equivalent of Shakespeare – that is what is most offensive. Without actually saying so, the programme is indeed an antidote to the 'all must have prizes' mentality. It is unashamedly meritocratic, judgmental, a living contradiction of the notion that all opinions are equally valid.

Dislike of the programme is widespread, and not confined to the ranks of the Conservative Party. *Today*, in another common criticism, is a programme that matters only to a self-selecting elite of media and political professionals. While the BBC in general has recognized the need to appeal to the whole of that ill-defined place called middle Britain and is working to do that, runs the argument, *Today* has become an incestuous little pond made and listened to by right-on liberals in north London. One such critic, Christina Odone, deputy editor of the impeccably liberal *New Statesman*, insists that the programme is 'very much about the chattering classes and the media'. Odone says she has never attended a newspaper editorial meeting at which *Today* was not discussed. She believes this media obsession with the programme perpetuates a myth that makes it seem more important than it really is. Journalists listen to it and write about it to the extent that even journalists who do not enjoy it feel obliged to tune in, just in case they miss something their colleagues will discuss.

Has *Today* become self-obsessed, a parody of its former self? Was it ever as good as the British media establishment insists it has been? Certainly the programme has had to adapt to retain its status – though it has always done that, as a work in progress, reinventing itself for each new era.

This book investigates how the programme achieved its unique status and how it manages to define the parameters of British political and public debate, on everything from the annual budget statement to the crucial question of whether domestic cats should be shot on sight to prevent further depletion of the songbird population. It asks how a programme that first woke Britain nearly half a century ago has managed to skip a media generation, make an ally of new technology, and remain essential in a way which suggests it will still be around in twenty years' time.

If *Today* is a programme for snobs, luvvies and the media aristocracy then there are an awful lot of them – some 6 million over the course of every week. The politicians who criticize it most violently know that. Despite all predictions that the glory days were over, during the general election campaign of 2001, *Today* remained the focus of political debate. It interviewed all the party leaders and infuriated the Prime Minister's press secretary by refusing to have its editorial agenda written in Downing Street. If it is incomprehensible to the majority, it is still essential listening to those who shape majority opinion. No other programme on radio or television can make that claim.

The Early Years of Today

S omething called *Today* made its first appearance before the British public at 7.15 a.m. on Monday, 28 October 1957. Harold Macmillan was Prime Minister, national service was still in force, John F. Kennedy had not been elected President of the United States and France's war time hero, Charles de Gaulle, was still nurturing a historic sulk at Colombey les deux Eglises. Tony Blair was four years old and William Hague had not been born.

That first edition – or to be more precise editions, because the original version of *Today* consisted of two distinct programmes of twenty minutes' duration, the first broadcast at 7.15 a.m. and the second at 8.15 a.m. – contained an eccentric cornucopia of whimsy. No recording exists, nor has a copy of the script survived. We know that the presenter was Alan Skempton, an entirely forgotten figure hired from his regular position as a BBC Home Service announcer.

In the opinion of the critic Anthony Thwaite, who wrote a report on the programme for its first ever editor, Isa Benzie, Skempton 'linked the items genially and without straining'. These apparently included a review of 'gramophone records' released that morning, an interview concerning the sale of correspondence written by the late Louis Napoleon Bonaparte, and an interview with a 'passenger flying to Scotland on business'. The name of the passenger has not survived, although Thwaite's report suggests he (and it must certainly have been a man) was not familiar with this new-fangled broadcasting phenomenon. Neither the passenger, nor the pilot responsible for conveying him, had anything 'of interest' to say, and 'threw an immense weight' on the reporter who had to 'jolly them along in the most obvious way'.

Although the combined duration of both editions amounted to a mere forty minutes, this first *Today* included music as well as speech. There was a segment from the opera *Aida* and some controversial pop music too. The then cutting-edge vocalist Petula Clark occupied minutes that might nowadays be allocated to a cabinet minister. Anthony Thwaite thought Clark 'a terror', and his 'listening companion' was 'unprintable about this'.

It was *Today* in name but not as we know it. No controversy, no assertive interviewing, no idea that radio might set the nation's agenda. This original style *Today* was elegantly described in a song written by Richard Stilgoe to mark the programme's twentieth birthday in 1977. Stilgoe sang

> In 1957 when *Today* was young and green,
> It went out in two editions with a vicar in between,
> Who gave thanks for the first one and offered up a prayer
> That they'd get it right the second time the show went on the air

A few items of 1957 vintage have survived in BBC archives. Among them is one that, without quite meaning to, speaks volumes about how the programme and the nation have changed. It was not an interview but a talk by a frighteningly 'pucker' young woman who had just been presented at court, one of the last debutantes to be accorded the honour. She was Fleur Hanson and, in an accent that makes contemporary monarchy sound common, she asked, 'The real question is, "What's the point of it?"' Neither philosophy nor sociology were central to the curriculum at girls' schools in those days, and Miss Hanson was not entirely sure.

'Well of course it means you're out. I'm not quite sure what coming-out entails, except that it's OK to be seen at a nightclub, although that's a doubtful advantage too. Of course it gives point to the season.'

Indeed. Still, Fleur Hanson knew which bit she liked most. It wasn't sitting in cars on The Mall for 'simply hours' nor the other debs' dress sense: 'My dear, the clothes!' she bitched energetically. 'I suppose it isn't anybody's fault, but nobody knows any more what's fashionable and what's not.' The best moment came when she was formally presented to the young Queen Elizabeth: 'I was so overcome I curtsied to the four winds... I'd like to be able to explain what I felt. That was the moment the whole business was all about. But I can't. It was a blank, but it was a divine sort of blank.'

One almost imagines Jim Naughtie saying 'Quite. But try and define this blank for us.' But no. The only familiar aspect of *Today* vintage 1957 was the justification for its existence. This was a ratings driven launch. Greg Dyke would not have argued with the case made.

It seems highly likely that the germ of the idea that eventually became *Today* originated from the late, great Sir Robin Day. In typical Civil Service style the BBC of the time did not credit Day for his revolutionary proposal. His ideas were not referred to directly at the first recorded meeting about the programme that took place at Broadcasting House on Wednesday, 15 May 1957. But Day's fingerprints are all over the series of memos and private discussions that preceded this official birth.

In 1955 Robin Day was very low in the pecking order at the BBC. He was thirty-one years old, a temporary talks producer, and clearly considered by his elders and betters to have an unreasonable degree of confidence in his own ability. The confidence appears to have been justified. In July 1955 young Mr Day wrote an enthusiastic memo to his then boss, the BBC's Chief Assistant of Talks. He made it clear that he had already discussed the themes raised in it with several senior colleagues (thereby proving that he had not learned one of the most important rules of BBC life, as important now as it was then – namely, that if you wish to get the remotest credit for original thought, do not mention it to anyone who might contemplate stealing it).

Day's memo, written shortly before the launch of ITV, argued that the BBC had a monopoly on morning radio but was doing precious little to justify it. He pointed out that the 8.00 a.m. news bulletin on the Home Service had an audience of about 6.5 million – 13 per cent of the British population. But this isolated oasis of information stood alone in a desert of bland mediocrity. With the exception of the 7.00 a.m. bulletin (a smaller audience, due to the time of day, but an equally impressive share of those who were awake), the BBC was offering Britain music with its cornflakes, along with a weather forecast and the cloyingly twee exhortation to Christian observance, 'Lift Up your Hearts'. Day clearly considered it enough to paralyse an inquiring mind, and outlined a possible alternative.

The young Robin Day appears to have had the quiet, unassuming arrogance of one who has not yet encountered the cunning hostility of older, less able, employers. His memo included the devastating understatement that 'I realize this proposal may mean radical departures from existing practice.' 'It also raises difficult questions of staffing and organization,' he conceded, but, with the optimism of a true prophet, he concluded that 'these obstacles' were a 'measure of the opportunity open to Sound Radio at this time of day'.

Day's proposal was submitted under the heading 'New morning Talks Programme'. It suggested that the BBC should offer its large captive audience 'something intelligent and lively by way of Topical Talks, something more than the present succession of routine items, service talks and light music'. Warming to his theme he suggested 'a new daily morning programme under such a title as "Morning Review"', and recommended that is should include 'pithy comment and description of the sort found on the feature-page of newspapers and in the more serious diary column'.

He went on to suggest a series of 'things that might be included'. These ranged from an interview or report on 'an event occurring late the previous evening or some important news released overnight and heard for the first time on the morning bulletin'. There might also be 'comment on some event due to occur that day', and on the previous evening's sporting calendar. Day wanted the items 'linked, without scripted presentation, by a skilled broadcaster who would give the programme form and personality without intruding his own opinions'.

Day was unambiguous about the ratings opportunity. 'As Television advances,' he wrote, 'Sound Radio will find more and more that early morning programmes command its big audiences. These are now its big opportunity.' He then set out the statistical case:

> In the last three years the average audience for the 7 a.m., 8 a.m. and 9 a.m. bulletins has remained constant at 10%, 13% and 9% respectively, yet for the evening bulletins over the same three years the figures have dropped from 18% to 15% (6 p.m.), 13%

to 12% (7 p.m.), 10% to 7% (9 p.m.) and 14% to 9% (10 p.m.). This trend will obviously be intensified. Another point is that there is a steadily increasing audience to car radios. This element must be particularly large first thing in the morning when people are motoring to work. These people cannot read while driving. Why should we not offer them comment and description that the rail or 'bus traveller can read in his newspaper?

The Day memo contains a potent combination of insight and common sense. In the eyes of his superiors at the then ultra-cautious and deeply traditional BBC, it contained something even less palatable – a veiled, but still stinging, critique of the status quo for which they were responsible. Day referred to the existing morning output on the Home Service as 'bleak and barren. If something is launched on these lines,' he predicted, 'I am sure that before long we will look back to the present morning programmes with the same incredulity with which we now regard pre-1939 days when there was nothing, not even a news bulletin, until mid-morning.'

At the time, Robin Day's intellectual honesty and creative candour made him much better suited for the independent television sector he was destined to join. In 1955 he had not learned the depressing truth that hide-bound officialdom may implement change to save its own skin but it does not thank people who identify its weaknesses. They attract fear and suspicion in equal measure. What Day suggested calling 'Morning Review' and planned to staff with 'younger journalists and broadcasters' sounds like scientific reasoning today. In 1955 he was thinking well beyond his salary grade and risking the wrath of the starched nonentities above him who lived in a culture in which apportioning blame was more important than allocating credit. This was still the BBC upon which Orwell based *1984*, content to abide by the rule that it should not discuss on air subjects due to be debated in the House of Commons until the debate had taken place.

In this context Day's proposals merit comparison with John Lennon's acute observation that 'life is what happens to you while you're busy making other plans'. Day's 'other plan' was the *Today* programme, but life took him to ITN first. Before he left, the future Grand Inquisitor tried again. He had received no formal response to his first memo so, just one week later, he wrote a second. That led to a meeting at which Day explained his idea to a herd of Home Service Producers. They professed to hate it, but there is good reason to believe that at least some of those present paid careful attention. If they did not, then osmosis must claim another of its mysterious accomplishments, because two years later they implemented many of Day's detailed suggestions.

To the extent that archives can express an opinion, the BBC's suggest that *Today* was the brainchild of the Marriott committee, a corporate panel which sat between 1956 and 1957 to chart a future for radio. But Day's idea had probably been filed away for use at a more opportune moment and was unlikely to generate original ideas without external stimulus. It is illuminating that, in a culture in which credit claiming was, and still is, rife, nobody has ever staked a claim to be the inventor of the *Today* programme. By the time the programme had established the foundations of its modern reputation, Robin Day was too modest and too accomplished to bother. He simply revealed the existence and contents of his 1955 memoranda and left it at that.

In any case, the creative origin of the programme matters very little in the modern context. The thing called *Today* that was launched in 1957 under the austere editorship of one Isa Benzie bore as little resemblance to the phenomenon Britain has come to know and love as a Trabant does to a Rolls-Royce. Benzie, a veteran BBC manager, was, until 1937, the Corporation's foreign director. At the time this made her one of only two women ever to head a BBC department. But her exalted status did not last long and ended for solid chauvinist reasons. An internal rule dictated that husband and wife could not both be employed simultaneously, and Benzie had married a colleague. She had to go, and was only allowed to return when the married couples ban was abolished in the post-war dawn.

One fact is unchallengeable. The title used by the *Today* programme was Benzie's idea. We have this on no less an authority than that of her boss, Janet Quigley, a chief assistant in the BBC's Talks Department. In May 1957 Benzie had written to Quigley enthusiastically proposing herself as 'organizer' of the programme mooted by the Marriott Committee. Benzie referred to it as 'Morning Miscellany', and her obsequious plea for appointment was tempered only by her effervescent girls' school language.

'Morning Miscellany' would need 'lots and lots of fresh ideas,' Isa Benzie was gushingly certain (and probably lashings of ginger beer too). 'Let's make this programme fairly full of things we've never done before,' she concluded. 'Let's give it character and do a splendid new service.' Reading the memo in the twenty-first century one anticipates a response along the lines of 'Dear Isa, you have always been my favourite prefect and it would be simply smashing if you would agree to take the lower fourth for morning broadcasting.' Other examples of correspondence from Quigley to Benzie are only marginally less Chalet School in tone. Miss Benzie (she appears to have kept her maiden name for professional use) must already have been offered the job because, in July, her boss put it on record that from a range of suggested titles including 'Morning Miscellany', 'Background to shaving' and 'Up in the morning early', Quigley professes to prefer 'Miss Benzie's simple "Today", with some such sub-title as "A radio magazine for early listeners".'

The BBC archives do not say so but the new programme was substantially the one Robin Day had proposed two years earlier. A document entitled 'Notes on Today' written by H. Rooney Pelletier, Controller, Programme Planning, Sound, just before the launch date borrows heavily from Day's ideas and justifications without any reference to their source. 'The programme,' Pelletier explains, 'completes the first stages of a planning pattern designed to give the listener a true alternative before 9 a.m.: the Home Service being mainly spoken word and the light Programme almost continuous light music plus time checks.' 'Today,' he goes on to say, 'is a collection of brief items, all of which can be said to have a topical interest for the average, intelligent reader of morning newspapers. It is seen as a logical follow up to the two news bulletins broadcast at 7 a.m. and 8 a.m.'

This may have been the era of Elvis Presley and Buddy Holly, the time when post-war austerity began to give way to modernity with all the associated phenomena of rebellion and the death of deference – but no one had told the Home Service. The original programme may occasionally have informed. It often entertained. It certainly did not challenge, infuriate or provoke. It took the best part of two decades for *Today* to find and fill that role.

At birth *Today*'s agenda was not politics, diplomacy and controversy but more food, health, music and whimsy. If the target listener was the intelligent newspaper reader identified by Mr Pelletier, then he meant, as Robin Day had suggested, the reader who concentrated on the features and diary columns. Archive records of the first year of programming suggest that even the items prepared for *Today* by the BBC's news journalists – as opposed to the Talks producers who staffed it – fell into the 'well fancy that' category.

Controversy appears to have been limited to internal concern about the choice of presenter. Again Day's revolutionary proposal that the programme should be presented by a skilled broadcaster with personality seems, by 1957, to have become the management consensus. But the notion that a presenter could be himself without intruding or sounding partial was still horribly new to a corporation that had once required radio newsreaders to wear formal attire at the microphone. Senior figures seem to have got themselves into a bit of a frenzy about poor Alan Skempton. The man was struggling to find the middle ground between cold formality and a degree of character. He did not get much of a chance. Some unscripted comment – presumably an attempt to inject the element of character – was deemed to exceed acceptable norms, and Skempton was replaced by a continuity announcer called Jack de Manio.

If Skempton's sin had been to allow too much of his personality to show on air, then de Manio was a very eccentric replacement. To many members of the *Today* audience his arrival marks the beginning of the programme's golden era. De Manio's name is still mentioned in the same breath as those of John Timpson and Brian Redhead, and there is no question that he had character and was enormously popular. But de Manio achieved what no modern presenter should ever be permitted to do. Between 1958 and 1971 the programme came to be perceived as his private domain. He was spoken of in the same adulatory terms as disc jockeys and entertainers. Personality had arrived with a vengeance and *Today* became Jack de Manio's show. To some fans it became simply *the* Jack de Manio show.

The modern *Today* presenter James Naughtie remembers the reverence in which de Manio was held. As a small boy, Naughtie used to fish a stream adjacent to a country house hotel in Banffshire. One day, friends from the village told him that 'a very important man' was staying at the hotel. Curious, he set out to discover who the mystery hero was. It was none other than 'Mr Jack de Manio of the *Today* programme'. Naughtie remembers being particularly struck by de Manio's fondness for whisky. The village was transfixed by gossip from the gillie who took de Manio fishing. The local man reported that the legendary presenter drank the stuff all day long and then returned to the hotel to drink more.

In an interview recorded after he departed *Today*, de Manio confirmed this fondness for alcohol. He regarded it as a partial, but entirely acceptable, explanation for his other famous failing – an abject inability to tell the time correctly. 'I never did it on purpose, I assure you,' he said. 'I found it terribly complicated at that time of the morning. You're interviewing somebody, you're thinking about what's coming on next and also you might have had a night out before, you're not in the best of fettle.' De Manio was truly execrable with clocks. 'For some extraordinary reason I can not account for,' one gem recorded for posterity has him saying, 'I said it was twenty-eight minutes past eight about two minutes ago. It's actually twenty-two minutes past seven. Please forgive me.'

On another occasion the presenter made himself, and a hapless colleague, sound even more absurd. 'From the *Today* studio,' de Manio declared, 'at just about [here there is a clearly audible sharp intake of breath] fifteen minutes... I can't read your writing. I've got a chap writing it out for me here, the silly fool, and I can't read his writing. Well, it's sixteen minutes to... and a half.'

Or there was the occasion – relentless efforts to locate it in the BBC archives have failed but everyone who worked on *Today* at the time insists it happened – when after an unscheduled hiatus at the start of the programme, Jack de Manio greeted his audience with an unexpected apology. 'I'm terribly sorry,' he announced to his adoring audience. 'I was on the loo.' *Today* had been on air for two whole minutes – but not in the form listeners were accustomed to. The newsreader had turned up in the studio at the appointed time. The technical team was in the cubicle along with the duty editor and the studio producer. The presenter was nowhere to be seen. Frantic phone calls to the office had no effect. Jack had left in plenty of time to reach his microphone. He just hadn't arrived. Frozen panic turned rapidly into action. There was no choice. Someone had to start the ball rolling. So the newsreader just launched into the opening summary by introducing himself and pushing ahead. Most people would not have noticed the difference if de Manio had not decided to offer his explanation. But that wasn't his style. He told the world. As the *Guardian* columnist Polly Toynbee wrote on 24 April 1999, anyone who thinks that *Today*'s early years must have been its golden era 'should have a salutary listen to one of Jack de Manio's atrociously trivial old programmes'.

Another example from the archive includes a lengthy chat between de Manio and a very articulate public school boy called James Showers. Master Showers had come to the programme's attention because he had hatched a duckling from an egg by keeping it under his arm for three solid weeks. Among the incisive questions put to him by de Manio are, 'What about games?', 'What did you do when you were playing cricket?' and 'How did masters react to you going around with one hand tucked under your arm all the time?' He does not ask where the boy stole the egg from in the first place.

Still, the item is fun. Showers handed the egg to another boy when he was batting and reveals that he got the idea from a prisoner of war who hatched a raven's egg while in captivity. The modern *Today* programme would not report it in that form. A recorded package would be preferred, to include the boy, his teachers, matron (who wrapped the new born in cotton wool and put it in a cage with a hot water bottle) and expert comment on whether the duckling would survive.

The presenter during those early years was not the only problem but he was a big part of it. De Manio's capacity for spectacular errors of judgement extended to far more significant issues. His reactionary bias was sometimes transparent. One Monday morning in 1968, just after the Grosvenor Square protests against the war in Vietnam, de Manio greeted the nation with the words, 'Good morning. And let us begin this morning by raising our hats to the London policemen, who once again have had their weekends mucked up by a lot of silly hooligans.' The programme editor at the time, Stephen Bonarjee, defended his star on the grounds that 'Jack represented the views of the public at large.'

De Manio appears to have had equally old school views about the tide of female liberation that swept the nation in the late 1960s. In one famous 'mistake' he concluded a question to a female assistant prison governor by wondering whether 'the prisoners will regard you as a good screw?' His justification on this, as on many other occasions, was to insist it had been an unfortunate slip of the tongue. De Manio's popularity protected him from the consequences of such errors and, several veteran *Today* staff believe, encouraged him to commit more. Contemporary debate about his more outrageous errors of taste and judgement appears to have largely overlooked the possibility that he did these things on purpose, and considered the programme a private pulpit from which to preach his unreconstructed personal beliefs to a mainly tolerant audience.

Above all, de Manio was a performer, not a journalist. He does not appear to have regarded it as his role to make sure that he was fully and exhaustively briefed on the news agenda likely to be covered by the programme. Indeed, a note written by Stephen Bonarjee in 1970 in response to de Manio's request for more money reveals just how cavalier he was. Reluctantly agreeing to his prima donna star's demand for £8 for conducting an interview outside scheduled working hours, Bonarjee also notes that 'as he seldom keeps to his contract time of 6.30 a.m. he owes us hours of work'.

To someone familiar with the work schedules of modern *Today* presenters this is a fascinating revelation. Messrs Humphrys, MacGregor and Naughtie arrive at Television Centre between 3.45 a.m. and 4.15 a.m. to prepare for a programme which now begins at 6 a.m. De Manio's *Today* did not start until 7.15 a.m. (in 1963 the first edition was extended to run between 7.15 and 7.45) and was not as long as the modern programme, but until 1970 de Manio worked alone, not as one of two co-presenters. Despite the responsibility this imposed, and the stated desire of the programme editor to make *Today* less eccentric and more news-dominated, de Manio obviously regarded forty-five minutes as more than ample preparation. If it takes a veteran correspondent of John Humphrys' calibre two hours to familiarize himself with his brief, it seems hard to imagine how de Manio could achieve the same in less than half the time. The bald truth is that he couldn't, but did not seem to care.

The 1960s vintage *Today* that de Manio fronted with such verve and anachronistic panache did not take itself particularly seriously. That it should be presented by experienced journalists, intimately familiar with their subject matter, was an idea that did not become an absolute until the late 1980s – otherwise the BBC's post-de Manio experiments with figures like Robert Robinson, Barry Norman, Desmond Lynam, Ludovic Kennedy and Melvyn Bragg could never have occurred. But even in those gentler times, Jack de Manio lost the confidence of his employers long before he had the chance to make himself unpopular with the audience.

In 1971 he was eventually shunted off to the Saturday edition of *Today*, where he lasted only a few months before being dropped altogether. De Manio pretended his phased departure was because he was tired of getting up before dawn (which he must have done at least during the winter months); however, it was actually because the BBC was finally beginning to realize what *Today* could become, and Jack de Manio had no part in that future. He was a sweet old dinosaur from a bygone age, and news and current affairs broadcasting was beginning a long and painful struggle into the present.

Despite a variety of hurdles placed in its path by the BBC, *Today* had been a ratings success throughout the 1960s. Regardless of assorted regional opt-outs (whereby listeners in certain parts of Britain heard local programming, particularly during the second edition of *Today*), the idea of early morning talk had won friends, and total listening figures amounted to between 3.5 and 4 million per morning. The programme team certainly realized that, despite the vagaries imposed by de Manio's manic eccentricity, they were dealing with something that had the potential to be important. That thought must have inspired editor Stephen Bonarjee to take advantage of the show's extended duration (introduced on Monday, 7 October 1963) to demand a new 'feel'.

Bonarjee recorded his thoughts in a memo to staff one month before the introduction of the new format. 'We ought,' he wrote 'to regard the extension of time ... as marking a new starting point.' He was clear about what this should mean. He did not want too many 'jolly magazine items' and required 'rather more roughage in the shape of sharper, harder material'. In a very small way it was the formal beginning of *Today* as a serious journalistic outlet. He wanted a more polished and professional approach: the programme 'should have a forward-looking feel about it, should concern itself mainly with broad extrovert human interests and talking points'. He was keen that his team should keep the ethos 'lively', while not being afraid 'to be serious when necessary (although hardly ever solemn)'.

A more significant step forward took place seven years later, when the veteran newspaper and BBC correspondent John Timpson was drafted in to co-present *Today* with de Manio. Timpson had been used as a stand in for several years and had won glowing reviews from Bonarjee. But it was the decision to use two presenters simultaneously that allowed Timpson to establish himself. De Manio must have realized his reign was nearing termination when he was obliged to share the job. Nor can it have escaped his attention that Timpson was everything he was not – informed, judicious a journalist to his socks. De Manio was a performer who had sought to grasp the rudiments of journalism; Timpson was a reporter with personality. Co-presentation immediately offered a new and safer variation of 'character' to the unscripted portions of the programme. The presenters could talk to each other instead of spiralling off into personal opinion. It encouraged the banter for which *Today* has become legendary. The advantages were noticed immediately by the BBC. Since the first time John Timpson joined Jack de Manio at the microphone, *Today* has always been a co-presented show.

John Timpson was not a political specialist like Jim Naughtie or John Humphrys. He enjoyed what he called 'the lighter side of *Today*' as much as the serious news agenda. Many listeners remember him for his attempts to interview a singing cat (called Blackie), an operatic parrot which was reluctant to perform, and other such trivial items. Brian Redhead christened Timpson 'the ho-ho man' and cringed inwardly at his colleague's sense of humour. On one occasion Timpson had read out with gusto a newspaper headline from the *Financial Times*: 'Insulation. Britain lags behind.' Redhead left a few painful seconds of silence before deadpanning 'Ho. Ho.'

Timpson was a compromise between the old, purely whimsical *Today* and the intelligent programme it was to become. He was perfect for the *Today* programme of the 1970s because that was a slightly uncomfortable mixture too. There was gravitas – for example, live presentation from the Common Market summit to consider UK membership. At Dublin Castle in March 1975 Timpson was to interview Prime Minister Harold Wilson. The presenter introduced the Prime Minister as 'smoking a mellow birthday cigar and in a mellow birthday mood' (European leaders had just serenaded him with a rousing rendition of 'Happy Birthday'). Then he got to the point and asked if Britain was joining the EEC or not. Wilson explained that the summit negotiations had reached a conclusion. He had just received the terms on which Britain would be allowed to join. 'Now the Cabinet will decide,' he said, 'and the people in a referendum.' Would Wilson advise the Cabinet to enter the Common Market or no, asked Timpson. Wilson replied, 'I think I'll put it to the Cabinet before I put it to anyone else.' The item was an early example of a minister refusing to make policy on the *Today* programme and then proceeding to do just that. Wilson was known to favour British membership and Timpson asked if he would accept the Cabinet consensus if it was different from his own opinion. Such a discrepancy 'doesn't usually happen', replied the Prime Minister – making it clear that he would advance the case for membership and encourage his colleagues to support him.

A few weeks later came an amusing interview with the new Conservative leader Margaret Thatcher. 'We've always been a party which has recognized that Britain has a future in Europe,' she told *Today* listeners on 17 April 1975. 'Britain can represent the Commonwealth in Europe. It would be absolutely wrong of us to play politics with that and say, "Because we could topple the present government, we're going to be anti-European." Oh, fundamentally wrong, and I couldn't possibly do it.' How things change. *Today* was changing too. Politics was slowly taking up more space in the mix. Occasionally this allowed Timpson to combine the serious with his love of levity. A marvellous moment occurred during the 'winter of discontent' when a Conservative MP, Joseph Kinsey, voiced his objections to a gas board advertisement which advised customers to save energy by sharing a bath – suggesting that the experience might be pleasurably romantic. 'It might be alright for the trendy south,' opined Mr Kinsey firmly, 'but we don't want it in Birmingham.' Timpson began his interview by asking Joseph Kinsey if he was in the bath.

'No. I can't get in the bathroom. I've got a teenage daughter.'

'On her own, presumably,' replied Timpson.

There was a moment's pause. 'I hope so,' said the MP.

Though *Today* was improving, it was not certain of its identity or function. The 1970s witnessed excruciating experiments like 'Keep fit with Eileen Fowler'. It is hard to describe the sheer inanity of this early version of radio aerobics, but here is a flavour:

> Do you think you could possibly stop what you are doing just for a couple of minutes? Helen's at the piano and Roy's our organist and then we can all do it to music. Are you going to? Fine. Come on then. Come out into the middle of the room. Stand with both feet together. Stand tall. By that I mean lift the chest – that's it: tummy in, head up, eyes level. Now, see what it feels like if you sag. Just drop. Awful, isn't it? Tummy comes out, chest all flat...

More embarrassing still to revisit were the particularly eccentric Saturday morning editions. An example from October 1972 has Michael Aspel introducing Silvino Trompeto, chef at the Savoy Hotel in London. Aspel reveals that Silvino is going to share his recipe for 'soufflé surprise aux pêches'. The chef takes a patronizing moment to congratulate the presenter on his French accent – 'Very good, Michael. Very good indeed' – before listing his ingredients. Saturday was supposed to be light, but this was gossamer.

The constant throughout this time was John Timpson. Bud Evans, a veteran *Today* producer, recalls an occasion when the British Rail train Timpson was taking to the Social Democratic Party Conference broke down in Cambridgeshire, somewhere near the town of March. Timpson was not familiar with the territory, or at least pretended not to be. On the guard's announcement that the delay 'will not be too long – we will get a new engine in March', Timpson sat bolt upright. 'March?' he squawked. 'It's October and I've only got one bottle of whisky!'

That cameo encapsulates the early ethos of the *Today* programme. Until the dawn of the Thatcher era, it was a quirky, bluff, endearing institution, content to be popular but rarely challenging. Its success was in its warmth and eccentricity, not in its ruthless agenda-setting. Britain had been governed since 1951 by the Butskellite consensus according to which governments of left and right exchanged power at elections but aspired to change very little else. The decline and fall of the Labour administration, led first by Harold Wilson and then James Callaghan was to end all that. The arrival of ideology as the driving force behind government would also change *Today*.

The Golden Years

T he partnership which began to shunt *Today* towards the modern era was born in the autumn of 1975. Monetarism had not been heard of and the monolithic Soviet state still looked potent, threatening and unshakeable. The new arrival, a product of Newcastle Royal Grammar and Downing College, Cambridge, would go on to preside over *Today* for nearly two decades of revolutionary change in world and domestic affairs. What listeners noticed first about Brian Redhead was his remarkable chemistry with John Timpson.

Like Timpson, Redhead was a journalist and a spectacularly good one. He had been editor of the *Manchester Evening News* and of the northern edition of the *Guardian* – although he routinely dropped the words 'northern edition' when speaking to impressionable young producers.

The relationship between Timpson and Redhead came to be adored by listeners and critics alike. Their combined on-air presence gave the programme warmth, sparkle and gravitas. Every variety of superlative was used to praise it. But they had little in common. Theirs was a brilliant performance that concealed the truth that they never became friends and nurtured an intense and often bitter rivalry.

Brian Redhead was an arrogant man. He had no intention of learning from John Timpson – indeed, rarely acknowledged that there was anything at all he needed *to* learn. I remember a quiet morning in the *Today* office when Redhead, not impressed by the programme running order – there weren't enough exciting live interviews for him to conduct – was engaging in his regular pastime of proposing a series of items the programme team ought to have thought of themselves. Banging his old manual typewriter in frustration (he never adapted to computers),

Redhead held up a copy of the *Guardian*: 'Now that's a good story. Get the minister on and I'll grill him about it.'

It was the height of the Thatcher era and the story was a tale of woe about men cast aside by the decline of the manufacturing industry. The *Guardian* ran a finely crafted newspaper feature, which made excellent reading but revealed nothing new with which to confront a politician. Duty editor that night and only twenty-seven years old, I made the mistake of pointing out that newspapers had room for that sort of colour writing but *Today* did not. Redhead regaled the team with a tale of when he was 'running the paper'. In those days he didn't have to put up with the opinions of mere twenty-seven year olds. He got what he asked for. I didn't argue. The prospect of the nation's favourite radio presenter walking out or going on air in an irascible mood was terrifying. I went out for a smoke; when I came back, Redhead looked up from his typewriter: 'So, have you fixed the minister for me?' Neither the minister nor his press officer, I suggested, would appreciate a pre-dawn call about a newspaper feature to which they would certainly not respond. Redhead turned to the programme assistant: 'Get me the bugger's home number and I'll call him myself.'

He didn't, of course. It was just his way of imposing authority. If Brian Redhead had been allowed to edit *Today*, the programme would have been a constant stream of senior politicians lined up for interrogation by the master. No news justification was required. He was sublimely certain that the nation wanted to hear him in conversation with people he considered his equals.

It could be infuriating, and occasioned endless bust-ups, but Redhead's confidence was part of what made him great. Asked to deal with a complex breaking news story at twenty seconds notice, he brought knowledge, insight and formidable clarity to the topic. He was unflappable on air and relished a challenge. His very presence encouraged adventurous journalism. Knowing that Brian could make it work removed doubt. And he was not just intellectually impressive. His humanity made him the perfect choice to interview the bereaved, nervous or inarticulate. Brian Redhead could put a child at ease as happily as he could skewer a dissembling minister. He could be ruthless, but usually when it was deserved.

At other times he simply charmed and beguiled. Many listeners insist they remember the morning that Brian Redhead was interrupted by the cleaners. It was shortly before 8.00 a.m. Everything was going smoothly and the great man was winding up the last interview before the weather forecast when Mrs Mop entered studio 4A with all the paraphernalia required for a thorough spring clean.

'Hello' she said to the bearded presence leaning towards a microphone, 'I've come to clean.'

'I think you'd better come back later,' replied a relaxed Redhead, 'unless you'd care to speak to the nation. This is the *Today* programme. It's live. Quite a lot of people are listening.'

To many fans the period from Brian Redhead's arrival to John Timpson's departure on Christmas Eve 1986 was *Today*'s greatest era, a period of consistent excellence to which it has never quite returned. Like the enormous affection that still exists for Jack de Manio that is rose-tinted retrospection. By the mid-1980s *Today* certainly was good, and Redhead's genius as a presenter was vital to making it so, but the process of change was not smooth. The programme's evolution mimicked the epochal developments then occurring in British politics.

James Callaghan's folksy, avuncular approach had proved no match for rampant inflation, rising unemployment and zero economic growth. He often seemed determined to prove the accuracy of a diary description of him written in 1956 by his predecessor Hugh Gaitskell, as 'a most talented Parliamentarian and a man of very considerable charm' but with 'absolutely no philosophical basis'. Outgoing Prime Minister Callagahan finally grasped the extent and nature of the revolution just hours before the election result was confirmed in May 1979. 'You know there are times,' Callaghan declared, 'perhaps once every thirty years, when there is a sea-change in politics. It then does not matter what you say or what you do. There is a shift in what the public wants and what it approves of. I suspect there is such a sea-change – and it is for Mrs Thatcher.'

If Callaghan recognized what had happened, he did not know how to respond. Nor did the *Today* programme. The years from 1975 to 1979 were a time of bleak confusion for the British left and for breakfast radio. In Brian Redhead *Today* had found the perfect chronicler of political change but it did not know how to use him. In the *'fin de siècle* atmosphere' which preceded Mrs Thatcher's determination to 'elaborate a new approach to reviving the British economy and nation', under a new editor, Mike Chaney, the programme began to experiment.

Chaney, a veteran of Radio One's *Newsbeat*, was determined to take his programme out of its metropolitan heartland. The plan was to capitalize on the potential of the Redhead/Timpson partnership as a north/south combination. This suited Redhead who had no permanent home in London. In April 1976 *Today* began what the BBC called 'inter-city' presentation, with Redhead in Manchester and Timpson in London. But if the idea was admirable, a sincere bid to bridge the north/south divide, the result was not. *Today* sounded disjointed. Repartee between the two presenters was crippled by the geographical distance between them, and the problem was exacerbated by one of those periodic bouts of self-mutilation to which the BBC is prone. *Today* was bisected, cut back into two editions at 7.10 a.m. and 8.10 a.m., with a trivial and disjointed thing called *Up to the Hour* jammed in the middle.

Chaney's editorship lacked the good fortune Lady Thatcher was later to enjoy. He wanted to make *Today* influential, a home for original journalism, but succeeded only in producing a mishmash, fronted by two enormously popular broadcasters and a rapidly changing coterie of deputies which included at various times Libby Purves, Nigel Rees and John Sergeant.

Failure was in any case preordained. Radio Four's incoming controller, Ian McIntyre, was involved in the traditional BBC activity of destroying everything his predecessor had considered sacred. His predecessor, the late Tony Whitby, had been enthusiastic about news and current affairs. McIntyre cut the hours dedicated to news programmes.

Brian Redhead told me he resented the period between 1976 and 1978 as a lost opportunity. The ideological influence of Margaret Thatcher's first guru, Sir Keith Joseph, fascinated him as much as the obvious intellectual vacuum at the heart of Callaghan's Labour government. Looking back from the vantage point of *Today*'s political influence in the late 1980s, he speculated about what the programme might have been able to achieve if the intellectual rigour it later brought to bear on political debate had been present then. Redhead even hinted that the bruising ideological battles between 1979 and 1987 might have been influenced if his full majesty had been brought to bear from the very beginning. Such imperious grandeur did raise a valuable point. The Chaney era at *Today* had recognized that change was coming, but the programme did not adapt sufficiently fast to reflect it.

Eventually Ian McIntyre was shunted sideways to become controller of Radio Three and Mike Chaney was kicked out too. In July 1978 *Today* was relaunched under the editorship of Ken Goudie. The disastrous London/Manchester experiment was abandoned and *Today* adopted a format that is still recognizable twenty-three years later. It started at 6.30 a.m. and ran through to the beginning of *Yesterday in Parliament* at 8.35 a.m.

Goudie's editorship created the skeleton on which his successors would build journalistic triumph. Presenters and producers alike felt that *Today* had been given the space and the remit within which it could grow to maturity. But there was still a lack of drive, and the atmosphere remained 'too relaxed, too clubby' according to one veteran still working on *Today* when I joined in 1988. 'There was still a complacency about it,' another former producer said. 'I think we thought that Redhead and Timpson were big enough in their own right – that if they talked intelligently about big events, it didn't really matter who they talked to.'

A review of the BBC archives for the period confirms that opinion. Even though James Callaghan's defeat has come to be regarded as the beginning of the modern era in British politics, the BBC's own cassette compilation of great moments from the first four decades of *Today* does not contain a single interview from the 1979 election campaign. The programme was reporting and reflecting but it was not creating news. That role was reserved for *World at One* and its colossus of a presenter, Robin Day. *Today*'s next two editors, Julian Holland and Jenny Abramsky, would emerge from the same academy.

Julian Holland arrived at *Today* in October 1981, just after the Toxteth riots but in time for Margaret Thatcher's first crisis.

Unemployment stood at over 2 million and rising. Inflation was higher than it had been under Callaghan. Thatcherism was assailed on all sides, and not least from within the Conservative Party. Precisely a year earlier the Prime Minister had told her party conference, 'You turn if you want to. The lady's not for turning.' When Holland arrived at *Today* it looked as if Thatcher might be given no choice. The world was in deep recession. Many in Britain shared the view of the Oxford academic R.W. Johnson who had prophesied that Thatcher's 'ship is heading due North for the Pole and will, ere long, encounter vast and fearsome icebergs'.

The Labour Party, meanwhile, had torn itself apart at a special conference held at Wembley in February 1981, after which the gang of four, David Owen, Shirley Williams, Bill Rodgers and Roy Jenkins, had broken away to create the SDP and Michael Foot had been elected leader of a fragmented Labour Party and thoroughly infiltrated by assorted Trotskyite sects. Politics were going to be bloody and fascinating, and Julian Holland was determined to make his show the best place for the British public to hear the arguments and personalities which would shape the future.

Before *World at One,* he had worked on the old broadsheet version of the *Daily Mail*. His appointment was a decisive break from the days when *Today* staff regarded themselves as radio producers not journalists. Peter Hobday, appointed by Holland to be the third member of the Redhead/Timpson team, remembers Holland as a true equal of a national newspaper editor. His philosophy was simple. He had great presenters and a substantial audience. For the former to make a fresh impact on the latter, *Today* required a stream of high profile interviewees whose utterances would influence events. It must ask them questions that would guarantee newspaper as well as listener interest.

Julian Holland's tenure from 1981 to 1986 coincided with fascinating and controversial events in Britain and abroad. Sceptics may argue that no journalist confronted by an agenda which included furious rows between 'wets' and Thatcherites, war in the South Atlantic and a close approximation to war at home with the miners' strike of 1984–85 could possibly fail. But until Holland's arrival, *Today* had been content to cast a magisterial eye over events, to pass comment, but he forced the programme to engage in the national debate as an active participant.

Julian Holland made few serious mistakes at *Today*. The one for which he will always be remembered was the launch in 1982 of the Man and Woman of the Year Award. Holland should have listened to advice from professional opinion pollsters. They exposed the faults in his plan: no poll in which participants are entirely self-selecting and voting is not supervised can ever be entirely fair. At worst it will be exploited, at best simply meaningless. Man and Woman of the Year, and its successors, Personality of the Year and Hero and Villain of the Year, have consistently been both. If a section of the *Today* audience did not take part with such gusto, no programme editor would tolerate the administrative nightmare the competition creates for the programme team.

From launch Margaret Thatcher won the female section of the contest eight times in nine years. If that was the result of a finely tuned write-in campaign by local Conservative Associations, then they displayed a confusing lack of interest in the male candidates. Mrs Thatcher found herself partnered by male winners who included her bitter foe Arthur Scargill and arch enemy Bruce Kent, the General Secretary of the distinctly non Thatcherite Campaign for Nuclear Disarmament.

The poll was abandoned in 1991 after incontrovertible evidence emerged of orchestrated cheating on behalf of Lal Krishan Advani, leader of India's Bharatiya Janata Party, a figure most *Today* listeners obviously did not recognize. As one producer puts it, 'I suspect only a handful could have spelled his name.'

That should have been the end of an exercise fraught with difficulties. But the publicity generated by the contest got *Today* mentioned in every newspaper in Britain. During the Advani fiasco the publicity had extended to Delhi. So in 1994 *Today* allowed hope to triumph over experience and relaunched the competition with new technology. Listeners would nominate candidates by letter but would then vote electronically via a freephone number. The flood of photocopied voting forms would end.

For two years the new method seemed to be working. Then

in 1996 dozens of obviously suspect nominations arrived for politicians. The maverick MP for Billericay in Essex, Theresa Gorman, had at least one fan daft enough to send a couple of dozen letters of nomination in identical handwriting. In the *Today* office a producer sang the Ian Dury song 'Billericay Dickie', belting out 'I'm not a blinking thickie, I'm Billericay Dickie, and I'm doing very well.'

It was an optimistic prediction. Mrs Gorman's supporters were sweet amateurs compared to the Labour Party activists who orchestrated a campaign on behalf of their new leader, Tony Blair. Seventy-two hours after voting started, *Today* pompously declared that 'an organized attempt had been made to distort the vote. A spokeswoman told the *Guardian*, "they were all at it".'

They certainly were. If this was one of the few examples of common practice to unite supporters of Mr Blair and Mrs Gorman, they were not remotely lonely in their gamesmanship. Some political activists had sent chain e-mails that generated automatic nominations from every friend, colleague or associate who received one. The poll was banned again. Staff hoped that this time it would never be resuscitated.

Again the publicity potential was allowed to overrule common sense. Four years later, in December 2000, headlines like 'Nasty Nick puts heat on Pope in Today Poll' revealed that the contest was back again and in yet another new guise. Politicians would not be allowed to enter. This would be the *Today* programme 'Hero and Villain of the Year Awards'. Anne Robinson, quizzmistress on *The Weakest Link*, was the only woman nominated in either category, as a villain. The controversial Chief Inspector of Schools for England and Wales, Chris Woodhead, enjoyed the unique distinction of being nominated in both categories. He got only 12.8% of the votes in the hero section – half the number that elected him as villain of the year against stiff competition from Bob Ayling of British Airways and Brian Souter of the Stagecoach bus and railway group (nominated for his ferocious hostility to the repeal of Section 28, the notorious subsection of local government law introduced by Mrs Thatcher that forbade schools from 'promoting' homosexuality).

The entire exercise seemed calculated to provoke accusations of naked populism and dumbing down. There was still no convincing evidence that the voting was not being orchestrated. Did NUT officials encourage members to embarrass Woodhead? How did Souter, a man whose prominence was confined to Scotland, where *Today*'s audience is small, manage to attract such attention? The BBC maintains *omerta* on these issues. The poll generates publicity, and no matter how many listeners regard it as a form of popular democracy, that is really why it survives. Fans might argue that Julian Holland identified an inspired mechanism for generating free advertising.

The final transition from *Today* as a charming accompaniment to tea and hot toast to *Today*, the programme which transfixes cabinets and must be recorded at 10 Downing Street was completed by two new programme editors, Jenny Abramsky and Phillip Harding. Abramsky was appointed editor in March 1986, after Julian Holland had passed his statutory retirement date. For the previous five years she had been editor of *World at One*. The lunchtime programme had shaped her judgement as much as Julian Holland's.

'When I joined the BBC in 1978,' recalls Frances Halewood, deputy editor of *Today* between 1987 and 1996 and a member of Abramsky's team at *World at One*, '*Today* was hardly a political programme. *World at One* was much more incisive, more overtly political. But there was a sea-change in the late 1980s. From 1987 onwards it was probably the most important political platform in the UK. We had massive events: the collapse of the Soviet Union, horror in Northern Ireland, the fall of the Berlin Wall, and, at home in Britain, a governing party changing the rules by which Britain had been governed since the war and, simultaneously, tearing itself apart in a series of perpetual crises.'

John Timpson, meanwhile, had started to feel out of his depth under Julian Holland, whose new approach had revealed Brian Redhead's potential as an interrogator and John Timpson's unsuitability for the task ahead. Audience nostalgia for the Redhead/Timpson partnership owes more to affection for two great characters than hard editorial judgement. Timpson was certainly engaging. He was warm, familiar and fun. While he remained at the microphone, *Today* had begun the journey towards importance. But it had not properly arrived. Now he was adamant that he did not appreciate the dominance of political news. He took an early opportunity to inform Jenny Abramsky that he would retire at the end of the year. Like de Manio before him, he told the press that he wanted a break from pre-dawn work and intended to spend more time with his wife. In his case the explanations were at least partially true – but it is clear that his desire to rest was prompted as much by the changing agenda. Despite his own background in journalism, Timpson didn't like the ethos that wanted to make *Today* a truly heavyweight show. He was a reporter from the old school, more interested in explaining facts than challenging opinions. *Today* was deliberately moving from reporting news to actively seeking to make it. Timpson found the prospect depressing.

'The programme did get a bit more solemn,' he told Paul Donovan, author of *All Our Todays*, 'which was one reason that I was not sorry to leave, but decided to leave. It wasn't the fun it used to be.' But Timpson knew Redhead did not feel the same way. Redhead, he explained, had never shared his love of banter or levity. 'Brian thought it was a waste of time. He felt the airtime would be better employed talking to a politician.'

Frances Halewood remembers the arrival of Abramsky and the harder, political agenda with much greater affection. '*Today*'s golden era,' Halewood believes 'had nothing to do with Brian Redhead, John Timpson or John Humphrys. It was the direct result of Thatcherism and John Major's premiership at home and the end of the cold war abroad. Politics had become dramatically exciting. It wasn't just that serious journalists were interested in serious events. Important things were happening and the *Today* audience wanted to hear about them, wanted to understand why they were happening.' He recalls a subsequent conversation with Brian Redhead shortly after the resignation of Margaret Thatcher in which Redhead, with atypical modesty, said 'It was a real privilege to be a journalist under Margaret Thatcher. Every day something interesting happened.'

Newspapers, though, treated the departure of Timpson as the end of an era and considered it a significant blow to the programme's standing. The team assembled under Jenny Abramsky was more optimistic. *Today* was headed down the road pioneered by *World at One*. It would aspire to the gravitas achieved on that programme by broadcasters like Robin Day and William Hardcastle. Abramsky explained her philosophy to Paul Donovan in *All our Todays*: 'Julian Holland is one of the greatest editors I've ever known. He had given the programme a very clear focus and made it far tougher. ... I thought my job was actually to move it to where I think it is today. I believed it had to be *Today* not Yesterday, and that to do a programme that just reflected what had happened rather than took everything forward would be wrong. Our job was to set the agenda. As you woke up in the morning, you almost made the newspapers redundant because we'd taken it on from the newspapers. Having edited *The World at One* I had spent most of my time trying to show that we had a better judgement than *Today* and to out-do them in terms of the big issues. When I arrived at *Today* I said, "Right, we're now going to make life almost impossible for *World at One.*"'

Despite Holland's achievements, *Today* was still lightweight when compared to its lunchtime competitor. Jenny Abramsky's editorship lasted only nineteen months before she was promoted again, but in that brief time she set the standards which made *Today* essential listening. One of her most important decisions was the appointment of John Humphrys as a permanent replacement for Timpson. It was an inspired choice. A veteran of the Vietnam war coverage, formerly BBC Television's Washington correspondent and then a television newsreader, Humphrys' experience as a foreign correspondent and his detached cynicism towards politicians made him the perfect presenter for the challenges ahead.

Between 1986 and 1992 the world changed more fundamentally than at any time since the defeat of the Third Reich. Glasnost and perestroika in the Soviet Union led to the collapse of a superpower and the end of the alarming schism between NATO and the Warsaw Pact. Small nations re-emerged, first in the Baltic and then across central and eastern Europe – sometimes peacefully, as with Czechoslovakia's 'velvet revolution', occasionally with great violence, such as that which attended the overthrow of communism in Romania. The nations behind the Soviet security cordon threw off absolutism and looked with puzzled awe at the prosperous democratic west they had been taught to detest. It was an enthralling time to be a journalist and *Today*'s new presenter relished it. John Humphrys' own years on the road had given him a distinct empathy with those young *Today* staff sent off to report from uprisings, revolutions and civil wars.

Margaret Thatcher emerged from her third successive election victory stronger than ever and ready, as she put it, 'to put the world to rights'. That meant sweeping privatization and economic liberalization, a full-frontal assault on the mixed-economy consensus. Brian Redhead relished the opportunities all this provided for infuriating ministers and pricking their pomposity. At his side the new presenter grew rapidly in stature.

Did Jenny Abramsky perceive all that John Humphrys was to become when she persuaded him to leave television news for the challenge of *Today*? Almost certainly not – but she did prove herself an excellent judge of talent as well as news. She had done the same thing by appointing *Today*'s first full-time female presenter, Sue MacGregor.

MacGregor is the longest serving member of *Today*'s presentation team. Like Humphrys, she joined full time in 1987 and at Jenny Abramsky's invitation. But she had been a guest presenter since 1984, combining *Today* with her regular slot on *Woman's Hour*, which, with her directness and her crystal clear diction, she did for fifteen years between 1972 and 1987.

Jenny Abramsky had a brilliantly balanced team of presenters by the end of 1987: the heavyweight charm and character of Brian Redhead, John Humphry's forensic interviewing and Sue MacGregor's bright, professional capacity to render the complex relevant. With the full-time team ably complemented by Peter Hobday, *Today* was ready to handle years of drama as war swept the Gulf and the Balkans and the poll tax proved a step too far for Mrs Thatcher. In addition, Jenny Abramsky ensured that *Today* would be broadcast on Saturdays, chopped 'Thought for the Day' down to manageable dimensions and coped with the pressures and demands of the 1987 general election.

When Abramsky was promoted again, her successor, Phil Harding, who remains a senior BBC executive, decided that from now on the programme would mark the card of anybody who was going to have an interest in the news and public affairs during the course of the day.

He devised a test for his editorial expectations. Each night he watched the *Nine O'Clock News* on BBC television. If there were any stories on that show, twelve hours after his own programme had ended, which had not been on *Today* that morning, he wanted to know why. If there were issues and events on the evening news that could have been analyzed or flagged up on *Today*, he was disappointed and felt that the show had missed a trick. He was also clear about the need to make news too – the 'big hitters', senior figures in politics, diplomacy, showbusiness or the arts, had to appear first on the *Today* programme.

'I spotted that this was a sort of virtuous circle – that if you got one on, other big hitters would see this was the sort of programme they should be on.' It didn't just go for politics: if there was a chance to get the Aga Khan on the *Today* programme then you got the Aga Khan. It might be someone like Princess Anne, Salman Rushdie or Henry Kissinger. 'You knew what was going to happen,' says Harding. 'The way that Britain works, these people then meet up later in the day and say to someone at Downing Street, "I was on the *Today* programme this morning – did you hear me?"'

Harding thinks the widely publicized association between the programme and the Prime Minister was particularly important – even if listeners only knew half the story, Harding says it's an overstatement to say that Margaret Thatcher listened to the programme regularly. 'I was told that, actually, what really used to happen was that Denis used to listen and then Denis would come downstairs after the programme and say to Margaret, "You've no idea what those pinkos have been doing on that *Today* programme. It's absolutely scandalous." And she would get all her knowledge about the programme filtered through Denis!'

Adamant that this account comes from 'a very good source', Harding nevertheless insists that having the Prime Minister's ear (even by proxy) was not enough. Between 1987 and 1991, Harding asserts, *Today* defined the art of the short-form confrontation with a cabinet minister or shadow minister. 'I was the person who introduced the research brief as to what we actually wanted. Brian Redhead used to more or less tip them in the bin, but John took them and used them. And that was where we started to build up this thing about quite relentless political interviewing. What you did was you were clear on which two or three questions you wanted to see pursued and you had the evidence to back them up. It wasn't a catch-all interview. Well, we changed the nature of it.'

Eventually Harding acknowledges that politicians got wise to this new, forensic approach to morning broadcasting. 'You know it was like American football. You have certain play moves, they have certain defences. You were then into the "I've got two or three messages and I'm going to put my two or three messages over" – but there was a very fertile period when we first did it. The other thing about having the big figures on was if there was a story breaking that morning then you always asked them about that as well. You got the first quotes from a big personality on the story of the day.'

And *Today* certainly garnered a reputation – one that saw it condemned from the platform at Conservative Party Conferences, satirized in *Private Eye*, bullied, cajoled and caressed by political press officers, and made it essential listening. *Today* had become a cockpit for agenda-setting news and interviews. Phil Harding no longer defined his audience by broad reference to newspaper reading habits. He was responsible for the journalism cabinet ministers (or their husbands) had to hear.

While acknowledging the vital importance of the political and journalistic audience – Harding admits he designed aspects of the programme specifically for them – he adds, 'When I arrived I thought it was a very London-centric programme. I was making it for the Chief Executive of the Health Trust in Birmingham, the head of a section at the Yorkshire bank in Leeds, a teacher or head teacher in Plymouth. I wasn't just making it for movers and shakers but for people who had an interest in public or civic life everywhere across the UK. I thought it also had to be about a whole range of things other than politics and I also thought it had to do original journalism.'

So the programme began to carry out its own surveys. When the poll tax became an issue, *Today* got the Chartered Institute of Public Finance and Accountancy to do a survey of every local authority in the country and how much they were going to put their rates up by. 'And, lo and behold, you got the figures several weeks in advance of any council announcement of what it was likely to be. It was about lifting up stones and looking underneath.' At the latter end of the Thatcher government, public services and the delivery of public services had become a real issue: Harding put reporters to work, not just shroud-waving but to find out how it was all working. What did the new management and structure in the health service actually look like from the inside? He wanted the big names, the big hitters, the global importance but also 'a lot of digging at the ground level'. It worked and Harding soon found himself confronted by a furious Conservative Party convinced that *Today*'s scrutiny of change meant it was guilty of systematic left-wing bias. The wall of his office is still decorated with a cartoon depicting Broadcasting House leaning to the left into a 'pink zone'.

Harding's editorship also made *Today* the combination of light and shade it had long aspired to be, delicately combining the agenda-setting ferocity of Jenny Abramsky with the warmth of *Today*'s earlier years. 'I used to look for stuff which would give the programme sound,' he explains. 'When it had rained for twenty days on the trot, Dominic Arkwright did a piece which had no commentary in it whatsoever. It was a sound montage of various things about the rain and the weather. It had a person in an umbrella shop saying how good it was for business. It had bits of music, it had falling rain, it had the BBC weather centre, it had bits of weather forecasts. It was a pure sound montage.'

And he tried to capture the mood of the era as Britain experi-enced unprecedented prosperity under the Lawson boom but struggled with its conscience over unemployment, poll tax, AIDS and war on European soil. He commissioned Allan Little to do a piece on chaos theory. Fascinated by the new technolo-gies confronting consumers as disposable incomes grew, he asked reporter Malcolm Brabant to do a piece on the amount of time people were wasting waiting for machines. 'This was at the time when the Vivaldi on the answer machine while you waited for option three was just coming into its own. The piece was about how much time you could waste in the course of a day just waiting at call centres, waiting for telephone answering machines, and how frustrating it was. It was a case of putting your finger on something that people were conscious about but hadn't articulated, so they would say "I heard that piece on *Today*. It really summed things up. Have you noticed that too?" That was always my test.'

But Harding did not just rely on the power of personal recommendation to spread the word about his beloved *Today* programme. He was ruthless about publicity, getting quotes from the programme picked up by the Press Association wires service, and attributed, so they quoted *Today*'s interviews, making sure they got tapes of the programme. The more frequently people heard the *Today* programme mentioned, the more they would want to be on it and feel confident of reaching a huge audience.

Harding made *Today* indispensable and gave it balance. Shortly after the 1992 general election he was replaced by Roger Mosey, the third former editor of *World at One* to get the job and a man many regard as the most relentlessly political editor *Today* has ever had. If Holland, Abramsky and Harding had made *Today* essential listening for politicians, colleagues suggest that Mosey did not understand that it was heard by anyone else. He pursued a more resolutely political agenda than any of his predecessors. It may have been a fair reflection of the news agenda, a period of high drama in domestic politics. John Major's shock victory in the 1992 general election was quickly followed by Black Wednesday and the prolonged death throes of Conservatism. As euro-scepticism erupted and the Tory Party's instinct for internal loyalty died a very public death, *Today* could rely on arguments within the ruling party for a diet of constant controversy. Sleaze, the Prime Minister's grotesquely misguided 'back to basics' campaign and a parade of ministerial resignations all added to the mix. *Today* would have had to be a very political show even if the Conservatives had been the only party in Britain. But as the Conservatives slowly committed political suicide, life on the opposition benches was also becoming interesting. John Smith took over from Neil Kinnock as Labour leader, established real democracy in his party by replacing the trade union block vote with the principle of one member one vote, and established a commanding lead in the opinion polls. After

Smith's tragically premature death, Clause Four was abolished under Tony Blair, and Peter Mandelson and Alastair Campbell established the most ruthless media machine British politics had ever seen.

Only one thing had a greater impact on *Today*. It was the death of Brian Redhead. The veteran star had been close to retirement, but his sudden demise occasioned national mourning and a cascade of heartfelt tributes. The daunting task of filling Redhead's shoes fell to John Humphrys, but that created a second vacancy, which many at *Today* thought should be filled by Peter Hobday. The BBC top brass did not, and that suited Roger Mosey.

During his time on *World at One*, Mosey had recruited and trained the former *Guardian* and *Scotsman* political journalist James Naughtie. The two had become exceptionally close friends, to the extent that Roger Mosey is godfather to Naughtie's youngest daughter, Flora. Mosey had long planned to bring Naughtie to join him at *Today*. Redhead's death provided the chance, and on 28 February 1994 the Scottish political specialist came aboard.

Today presenters usually start their careers amid controversy. Naughtie certainly did. First there was his nationality – the new boy received a lot of letters saying 'Get back to Scotland' (he has since claimed that 'most of them seemed to come from fancy addresses in Cambridge'). But Naughtie was controversial for editorial reasons too. In 1994 he was best known for an interview conducted on *World at One* with Labour leader Neil Kinnock during the run-up to the European elections of May 1989. This became known as the 'kebabing' incident, in which Naughtie repeatedly pressed Kinnock to explain Labour's alternative to a high interest rate strategy and Kinnock angrily refused to answer. Real controversy at the time centred around the BBC's decision not to broadcast the sections of the interview in which Kinnock lost his temper. Among BBC journalists there was widespread suspicion that these livelier elements were suppressed to protect Naughtie rather than Kinnock.

Mosey's choice was not popular but it was vindicated. James Naughtie was the political specialist *Today* needed at an intensely political time. His other interests have proved more than adequate to cope with the broader demands of *Today*.

Phil Harding created a dynamic *Today* programme for a revolutionary time. He finessed the ideas of his predecessors and added many of his own to create a team that covered domestic politics, world affairs and whimsy with equal aplomb. He also faced a sustained barrage of abuse from the Conservative Party, so proving the importance *Today* had assumed in British affairs. Breakfast television was beaten out of sight. The great and the good beat a path to Studio 4A at Broadcasting House, determined to test themselves under interrogation by Redhead, Humphrys, MacGregor and Hobday. *Today* had finally grown up. It had become the agenda-setter Harding's predecessors had set out to make it.

But there was to be no time for celebration. Almost as soon as the programme reached this height of excellence, it was exposed to a whole range of new challenges. Conservative domination of British politics was to be challenged and overturned. The emergence of the Mandelson/Campbell school of media-management would present acute difficulties for *Today*. So would the launch of rolling news on BBC Radio Five Live, the arrival of satellite and digital television, internal reform at the BBC and the impact of the internet.

Finally, after the election of the first Blair government in 1997, *Today*'s assumption that a single British news agenda could be set and directed from London was rendered naive by the advent of devolved parliaments and assemblies in Edinburgh, Cardiff and Belfast. The comfortable notion of one British establishment conducting one national debate was no more.

During the late 1990s *Today* struggled to retain its significance. The BBC appeared hesitant, unwilling to let its flagship show confront the future with confidence. Through no fault of their own, Harding's two immediate successors, Roger Mosey and Jon Barton, spent as much time dealing with the internal politics of John Birt's BBC as they did shaping and modernizing *Today*.

The editor charged with meeting the demands of a changing world was not appointed until 1998. He was Rod Liddle. We will consider his record later.

THREE

The Best Job in Journalism

W hen Brian Redhead left the *Today* studio on the morning of 7 December 1993, nobody on the programme dreamed it was for the last time. He had been in obvious discomfort for several months. But Redhead was a diabetic – everyone at *Today* was accustomed to him looking and sounding tired before he went on air. In the last months, however, his grumpiness sometimes verged on the supernatural. He would switch from silence to splenetic fury in a matter of seconds. Trivial problems, like the discovery that his beloved typewriter was two desks away from his normal seat, would instantly provoke cruel words. Colleagues were peremptorily instructed to go to the Broadcasting House canteen to get Brian some breakfast, when in the past he would have got it himself – and have stopped along the way to ask if anyone else wanted coffee or toast.

Broadcasting House was quiet in the hours between 2.00 and 4.00 in the morning. Redhead must have suspected that his slow, painful limp along the corridor could be heard by the production team. So he sang. 'He must have been in agony. He would never admit how ill he was. Not even to himself,' says one former colleague, Nigel Charters. 'So he sang these falsely merry tunes all the way to the door. He knew we could hear him coming.'

'He was in his mid-sixties,' says Peter Hobday, who co-presented *Today* with Redhead for many years. 'He was still getting up and doing three or four programmes a week. He was still commuting to the north [Redhead never moved from his home in Macclesfield]. Think of that just in terms of travel, pressure, sleep. A sixty-five-year-old diabetic, putting in the sort of hours that many young people would blanche at, and the intellectual demands being made to keep up to date with absolutely everything.' The steady approach of his statutory retirement date may have made him even angrier. 'I'm not saying he was past his sell-by date, but if there was a fourth ingredient which could make an old person tetchy, it is that just as you think you've got it all sorted and made your reputation and you're firing on all cylinders, it's all going to come to an end for some arbitrary reason. This idea that he was now sixty-five and had to stop was actually working to his bane. I think Brian, more than almost any of us, had become so closely identified with the job that the thought of being introduced as "Brian Redhead *formerly* of *Today*" didn't cheer him up.'

Brian Redhead did not want to retire. He wanted to feel better. He wanted to rediscover his enthusiasm for having that word in the nation's ear or, as he sometimes said when leaving the office to go into the studio seconds before transmission, 'toddling off to address the nation'. The talk of statutory retirement did not help. Redhead spoke of the idea quizzically or with bemused contempt. What was this nonsense about presenters having to go at sixty-five? He could name several who clearly had not. Alistair Cooke was still going strong. But duty editors would regularly allocate important political interviews to his co-presenter. One *Today* duty editor, now a senior BBC executive, routinely referred to him as a 'busted-flush'. Others gossiped about their wish that he would retire before he made himself look foolish. Discussion about the need to find a replacement was commonplace. The BBC did not want a presenter who was below par. Concern was focused on the product, not the man.

Peter Hobday was the presenter alongside Redhead in the *Today* studio on that last morning in December 1993. 'He seemed a bit distracted. He wasn't his normal, sharp self. I remember thinking "Brian's got to take it easy." I seemed to find myself not actually carrying the programme – you never carried the programme while Brian was around – but doing one or two interviews which were actually down for him because he just wasn't feeling like it.'

In the immediate aftermath of Redhead's death one question was to arouse passionate debate among his colleagues. Had the man whose name had become synonymous with the programme, to at least the same extent as Jack de Manio's, been allowed to work on when he was not fit? The BBC does not encourage this sort of discussion. It prefers to agree a party line and stick to it. But colleagues certainly knew he was pushing himself exceptionally hard to maintain his composure on air. A few feel guilty that he was not obliged to rest long before he went home to Macclesfield on 7 December 1993, planning to have an operation before returning to *Today* in the new year. It would probably not have been possible to persuade him, but it would have been nice if someone had tried.

The immediate cause of Brian Redhead's death in Macclesfield District General Hospital was a perforated appendix that poisoned his bloodstream and weakened his vital organs. Nobody, not even Redhead himself, knew about the problem. *The Times* subsequently devoted not merely an obituary but also a leader column to his passing, in which it acclaimed him as 'one of the most compelling figures in the glorious firmament of postwar radio'.

'In my view he was the best broadcaster in the country,' comments John Humphrys. 'He might have been the best broadcaster the BBC has ever had. You would have to be a complete prat – as he would have said – not to have learned from him.' For Sue MacGregor, who worked alongside Redhead for years, 'he was a born radio man. There have been different golden eras, but it's hard to beat any time in which Redhead was there for sheer listenability.'

Peter Hobday adored Redhead's intelligence and humour. He especially remembers a Redhead interview with the Conservative politician John Wakeham during the controversy over privatization of the electricity supply industry. 'Wakeham, despite his name, tended to put the audience to sleep. He was the most boring interviewee, really ponderous, and he was droning on, saying, "What I think in the present context, and on the basis of discussion with my Cabinet colleagues...", and Brian suddenly just stopped him. "You know, Mr. Wakeham," he said, "I've got the advertising slogan for you. One man. One volt."'

'I think that's where I learned a lot from Brian,' explains Hobday 'that you didn't have to shout. He was never vicious in his hard interviews. It was always irony or well-intentioned sarcasm when he didn't believe something, not the sort of argy-bargy approach that a lot of modern interviewers have got.

Brian always had a sense of humour. He got more letters about his "Friends of the M6" than any of his political interviews. It was what he meant in that great phrase about "having a word in the ear of the nation".'

During the Gulf War, Allan Little, now the apprentice presenter Redhead himself was when he first shared the *Today* studio with John Timpson, travelled to Baghdad for BBC Radio. He was in the Iraqi capital the morning that Allied bombs destroyed a bunker packed with 300 women and children. 'I was thirty-one and relatively inexperienced. When I got there they were still pulling the bodies out… I remember not being able to speak. So I just wrote notes. I thought, "Right, I'm going to have to go back and explain what I saw."'

Returning to his room at Baghdad's Al Rashid Hotel, Little filed a dispatch for BBC News. It was heard by a *Today* programme producer who realized the reporter had been an eye witness to something particularly horrible, and wanted Little to tell his story immediately. Brian Redhead asked him what he'd seen. 'I started to flounder. I couldn't get to the point. I heard myself saying "Well, there's a suburb of Baghdad. It's about half an hour from the centre. It's a middle class suburb. The sort of people who live there are school teachers…". And Redhead took control because he could hear that I was upset. It was like a big avuncular hand reaching out and landing on my shoulder. And it was only then that I managed to describe what I had seen.'

While always dignified and magisterial on air, however, in the office Redhead was an ill-tempered sprite. A provocative iconoclast, he could be blatantly offensive even to friends. Absent colleagues were condemned as 'bloody prats'. He routinely referred to Sue MacGregor as 'the Dowager Duchess of Dingly Dell' – but only when she wasn't there. 'I think a lot of people found Brian immensely irritating,' says MacGregor. 'He sounded too cheeky-chappy and too big for his boots. He could certainly be difficult to work with. He was fine to me at the beginning, but I think once another presenter had got their feet under the table, Brian didn't want anyone to threaten his *primus inter pares* position.' During one live interview, she remembers, Redhead wrote 'FOOL' in block capitals on a sheet of paper and thrust it under her nose. 'There was a very Walter Mitty-esque side to Brian,' reflects MacGregor. 'He embroidered the truth enormously. He'd invented almost everything and he'd been clever from the age of eight.'

Redhead did indeed gild the lily. He deliberately conveyed the impression that he had been the editor of the *Guardian* (rather than merely its Manchester edition), but still more childish was the misrepresentation of his degree result. Redhead was a Cambridge graduate – a fact he regularly paraded for general approbation – and claimed to have obtained first class honours. This was not true. Brian Redhead got a first in his second year exams but an upper second in his finals. By any normal standards that amounts to an upper-second class degree. Redhead routinely overlooked the final result. But he talked about his first in such peculiarly ambiguous terms that one of his colleagues took the trouble to check with the university. The discrepancy caused amused comment among the programme team. It was not mentioned directly to Brian. 'We all knew that was part of Brian,' says Sue MacGregor, 'that huge self-confidence. Anyone who is a personality with a capital "P" and who gets the sackloads of fan mail that Brian did is bound to be a little bit larger than life.'

Brian Redhead had a very simple sense of what news means. If he was broadcasting it, then it mattered. If he was not involved, it did not. Andrew Hawken, a former assistant editor of *Today* remembers an alarming case of rampant ego and *amour-propre* during a trip to Tokyo, where he and Redhead had been sent to produce a series of live contributions on the state of the Japanese economy. It had looked like an interesting idea when they set out, but, as often happens, the domestic news agenda blew up while they were away. After they'd already spent two weeks researching there, the duty editor in London explained that contributions from Redhead would not form a significant proportion of the next morning's programme. Hawken remembers Redhead shouting down the line, 'I'm going to knife you when I get back!' Then, five minutes into the first programme, Redhead's one item got dropped. 'He slammed down his headphones, got on the talkback and said, "Right. That's it. I'm not standing for this. Order me a cab to the airport. Go on – order it now!" and then he walked out.'

In fact, Redhead calmed down. He usually did. But not before he had caused everyone else to run around in blind panic.

But beneath this spiky exterior was a warm humanity and a compassion which close friends said had been deepened by the appalling death of his son, William, in a car crash in France at the age of only eighteen. At the end the BBC did not treat Brian Redhead as generously as it might have done. He left *Today* with a whimper, not a bang, and before his millions of admirers had the chance to tell him how much they adored him. Only Peter Hobday did that, in the tribute programme transmitted the morning after Redhead's death, with the heartfelt admission, 'I loved the man.'

Among the *Today* presenters of the time, Brian was the best. It wasn't argued about. He just was. Now the same status has devolved to John Humphrys. He is self-effacing about what it means to present *Today*. 'The honest answer is profile. You can do equally worthy programmes, but you haven't got an audience of millions listening to you. *Today* has an enormous audience and it has breadth of audience. It has every managing director and senior politician – but it also has taxi drivers. There isn't another programme like it in Britain, in the world, probably. Certainly there is nothing like it in the United States. It's very nice to be on a programme where you know you are going to talk to all of the movers and shakers pretty well all of the time. Pretty nice to be in the centre of events all the time.'

Sitting in his comfortable, family kitchen in a quiet but unspectacular enclave of West London, John Humphrys does not look like a man approaching the age at which most professionals would consider retirement. Tanned and dressed in loose fitting jogging pants, he is lean to the brink of scrawniness. Health matters to Humphrys to the extent that he can appear faddish, slightly obsessed with fresh foods and a carefully managed diet. He tries to drink a gallon of water before consuming anything else in the morning. He won't eat farmed fish and has been a proselytiser for organic produce since he briefly owned a Welsh dairy farm.

This sort of outlook is rare in his profession. Smoking and drinking are still common among journalists. Many are dead before they reach John Humphrys' age. But while he rejects many of their less appealing habits, John Humphrys still calls himself a hack, the bluntly dismissive journalist's name for a journalist. It can sound derogatory, or perhaps in his case, a manifestation of false modesty. The way Humphrys uses the term, it is neither. He is proud of his trade and happy to admit he enjoys it. In the introduction to his own book, *Devil's Advocate*, Humphrys made light of the risks he faced as a foreign correspondent and concluded 'most of it is great fun. I have yet to meet a moderately successful reporter who would willingly swap his job for another.'

Humphrys has reported for forty-three years. He started in 1958 as a local newspaper trainee in his native Wales and has used the core skills he learned there to convey news of many of the greatest events of the last half-century. He was in Washington when Richard Nixon resigned. He attended the party at which South Africa celebrated the election of Nelson Mandela as President. He covered the 1966 Aberfan disaster for HTV, the Welsh commercial broadcaster which gave him his first break in television after formative years on the *Penarth Times*, *Merthyr Express* and *Western Daily Mail*.

There is an endearing absence of pomposity about John Humphrys. He says, quite matter of factly, that he has got a chip on his shoulder. Nor does he give much impression of liking the rich, powerful people he often finds himself interviewing. He was one of five children born into a poor family in Cardiff, whose mother worked from home as a hairdresser and whose father, George, was a French-polisher with skills in a trade too few local residents required. John was certainly unimpressed when his father obtained work from affluent families and was requested to use the tradesman's entrance. Showing a fierce pride, which his son has inherited, George apparently refused, even when it meant losing the work.

Humphrys attended the selective Cardiff High School. He says he hated it and he left when he was just fifteen. He has never studied at university and sometimes shows a hint of hostility to those who think academic degrees matter. He does not object to reading, analysis or intelligence – indeed, he is extremely well-read himself. It is the cliquish clubability of many graduates he seems to find irritating. When I was a new boy on *Today*, Humphrys looked up from a copy of the *Daily Mail* and asked, 'Where did you go to university, Tim?' I told him I was a Cambridge graduate. He smiled, and looked back at his paper. 'Never mind. You seem quite bright.'

There is a powerful sense of the self-made man about John Humphrys, a conviction that because he had to work hard to achieve what he has, others should have to do the same. He rejects hereditary privilege and was openly dismissive of Robin Day for accepting a knighthood. He seems content to oppose anyone who exercises political power for the simple reason that he is suspicious of power itself.

Humphrys is the king of the *Today* programme. He could afford to relax, to present less often and to enjoy the company of his partner Valerie Sanderson and young son Owen. Instead he agreed to present *Today* five days a week during the general election campaign of 2001. His work ethic conveys the overwhelming impression that a lot is never enough. He presents *Today* and BBC Television's *On the Record*, writes a regular column in the *Sunday Times*, freelances for numerous other publications and has written two erudite and well-researched books. But on top of that he regularly presents awards at ceremonies, makes speeches and provides professional training for other journalists. Until it was deemed unacceptable, Humphrys was happy to offer media training to people who might conceivably have faced him across the desk in the *Today* studio. 'Surely everyone who has been poor worries about being poor again?' he pondered in an interview in the *Independent* newspaper. 'Money is security. Money is knowing if it all finished tomorrow, I wouldn't have to end up in some dingy place.'

If it all ended? His desire to earn reveals an endearing lack of confidence in his own ability. The poor little kid who has made it by dint of sheer determination, no matter how far he rises, he can never quite escape the suspicion that one day the establishment will take it all away. It must be why he works with such ferocious concentration and attention to detail, why he interviews the complacent and the powerful with forensic aggression. He wants to know what they have that he lacks.

James Boyle, the former controller of Radio Four, regards

John Humphrys as the best *Today* presenter ever. 'There's one particular reason for it. He's able to set up those adversary-stance interviews and pursue them without any kind of personal posturing or anything other than clean journalistic aims. He never, ever forgets the issue. He pares it down to essentials and he doesn't get involved in irrelevancies. He recedes his own personality to an absolutely admirable degree.' Humphrys says that he learned early on not to try to sound clever when Margaret Thatcher responded to his undergraduate-style question, 'Prime Minister, what is the essence of Christianity?' with the single word: 'Choice.'

But *Today* is not a single-presenter show. Its charm and character depend on the on-air relationship between two broadcasters. When the daunting task of filling Brian Redhead's shoes fell to John Humphrys, a second vacancy was created, and on 28 February 1994 the Aberdonian James Naughtie duly joined.

Today presenters usually start their careers amid controversy. First there was Naughtie's nationality – he received a lot of letters saying 'get back to Scotland'. He has since claimed that 'most of them seemed to come from fancy addresses in Cambridge'. But there was also the *World at One* 'kebabing' with Neil Kinnock – which James Naughtie still refers to as his worst experience on air. The unbroadcast segments of the exchanges – leaked by angry colleagues to the London *Evening Standard* – revealed an obvious personal relationship between Naughtie and Kinnock, and sounded more like a flare-up between friends than a clinical interrogation. The incident for Naughtie's enemies, most of them on the right of British politics, was proof that he is too close to Labour politicians, that he has never made the leap from ideologically committed commentator for famously left-leaning liberal newspapers to objective, impartial BBC presenter. But while the Kinnock interview may have revealed a degree of inexperience in a relative newcomer to news and current affairs broadcasting, it took place thirteen years ago and all the evidence suggests that James Naughtie learned his lesson well.

The snide attempts to identify him with the New Labour elite reveal an ideological reluctance to understand the man. Naughtie is an elder of the Church of Scotland who has continued to attend the Kirk's outpost in Covent Garden, London throughout his career at *Today*; he is a deeply traditional, some might say conservative, figure. Most criticism of him can be traced back to one bald fact: that he is, by his own admission, a 'political junkie. I got into political journalism because I never wanted to do anything else,' he says. 'You have to love the atmospherics of Westminster, the gossip, the characters involved, the way people shape policy and make decisions. You have to be fascinated and intrigued by it.'

This early career outside broadcasting marks him out from his colleagues, none of whom has ever faced the demands of national newspaper journalism – the constant pressure to obtain and reveal new information and new insights for an editor who starts each day staring at vast expanses of empty space. It was inevitable that Naughtie would make and nurture contacts with an intensity that most broadcasters do not, but this is proof of professionalism, not bias. Andrew Marr, the BBC's current political editor and himself a former newspaper reporter and editor, has faced similar criticism for exactly the same reasons.

Sue MacGregor joined *Today* full time in 1987 but had been a regular guest presenter since 1984 when she first began to combine her regular slot on *Woman's Hour*, which she presented for fifteen years until 1987, with appearances alongside Brian Redhead, John Humphrys and Peter Hobday. The *Today* website claims that she joined the BBC as a current affairs producer, which looks like a retrospective nod in the direction of equal opportunities. She didn't. She first came aboard as a secretary – a common tactic for ambitious female journalists in the rigorously misogynistic BBC of the 1960s – before getting a more senior job with the South African Broadcasting Corporation, taking charge of their women's programme for five years.

The South African connection is important. MacGregor was born in Oxford but emigrated when she was very young to Cape Town, where she grew up under apartheid. She did not go to university, except for 'a very brief term at the University of Cape Town' before going travelling in Europe. She has huge affection for her adopted homeland, of which her knowledge is encyclopaedic and says that one of her biggest disappointments was not being chosen to present *Today* from South Africa during the first post-apartheid election. John Humphrys got that assignment.

More than thirty years ago she got her big break at the BBC when she was appointed what she rather quaintly calls 'a girl reporter' on *World at One*. She excelled in the high-pressure atmosphere of the BBC's most serious current affairs programme at the time, and proved adept at the rapid turn arounds and fast, accurate writing it demanded. In the years that I worked with her I never felt that Sue was remotely interested in fame. Veterans who joined the BBC in the 1950s or 1960s used to draw a distinction between presenters and broadcasters. It was a bit like the old cricketing divide between gentlemen and players. Putting MacGregor in the broadcaster category was a compliment.

Sue MacGregor possesses a personal charm and politeness that harks back to a less casual era, is absolutely committed to radio as a medium, and has never adopted the male broadcaster's habit of bluffing instead of admitting ignorance. Slightly formal and reserved, she even seems reluctant to join in the social activities of *Today* staff. But she is no shrinking violet. Feisty in defence of her own position, she is exceptionally sensitive to manifestations of what she calls 'male chauvinist piggery'. As Paul Donovan revealed in his book *All Our Todays – Forty Years of the Today Programme*, MacGregor was incensed when she discovered that John Humphrys and James Naughtie were being paid more than her for doing the same job, and dogged in her pursuit of financial parity. A product of the women's liberation movements of the 1960s and 1970s, MacGregor cares about equality of opportunity and doing a good job, but not about joining traditional power structures. She has said that she is not comfortable with ruthlessness and once told an interviewer, 'I wanted to move on from being a secretary, but I never wanted to become more powerful in broadcasting. When I presented *Woman's Hour*, I had no desire to edit it.' An icon to many women of her generation, she was awarded an OBE for services to broadcasting in 1992 and later named 1998 Radio Personality of the Year by the organization Voice of the Listener and Viewer.

Sue MacGregor remembers the advice offered to her by Brian Redhead and John Timpson before her very first shift on *Today*.

'Timpson and Redhead took me out to breakfast. Redhead's advice was all about physical well-being and getting enough sleep and having a Zzzzz in the afternoon – which I actually followed. And don't drink too much the night before! Timpson's advice was more journalistic. I remember he said, "Once you're on the air there won't be a great deal of time to think and plan, so try and think up your strategy for the interviews before you go on air." So I always try to think of a decent first question and an ultimate goal for every single item before we troop into the studio at about two minutes to six. So that if someone says to you suddenly, "we're going to item 58 on the running order" when you've only got as far as item 12, you won't be completely flummoxed.'

'For me the real high pitch of stress is getting the writing and the preparation done before you go an air. I know Redhead once had something attached to him that showed that his heart, before he went into the studio, was doing that [she points towards the ceiling with both hands] and when he was on air it was like that [she demonstrates a completely flat trajectory].' But she offers a blunt warning about the perils of being too relaxed in the *Today* studio. 'I dropped off in the middle of an interview once and woke up babbling. It was only half a second of inattention and brain deadness but it was enough. It was very worrying.' The interviewee was a cabinet minister – she refuses to say who until she has retired. It will be a fascinating revelation. Which politician wants to be known as the dullard who bored a presenter to sleep before an audience of millions?

Sustaining a pitch of concentration every morning with such an early start demands a rigid adherence to routine. 'I get up too late,' confesses John Humphrys, 'just before four. I hold the world record for getting out of bed, into the shower, into the car, all of which can be done in about nine minutes. I'm three minutes from the office. So, I'm sitting behind my desk by twenty past four at the latest. My bum's hardly hit the seat before I've started to type. I type the introductions and all that sort of stuff. It fixes it in the head. And then I have a bowl of unsweetened muesli with a banana and skimmed milk. God, what a puritan! And read the papers. And that's it. Same procedure every morning.'

Humphry's ascetic sustenance is in marked contrast to a *Today* tradition in the early 1980s, when the programme had begun to grow up but journalists certainly hadn't, alcohol still being an essential component of any working day. For newspaper folk on what was then still Fleet Street, this meant liver-crippling draughts to be consumed at lunch time and after work. Special arrangements therefore had to be made for *Today* programme night shifts, since the 'Hat and Stick' (as BBC staff call the Crown and Sceptre pub behind Broadcasting House) closed at 11.00 p.m. So the whisky was introduced.

To begin with, this amounted to one bottle per week supplied by the editor. A line was drawn on the bottle to indicate how much could be consumed on each shift if the supply was to last a week (additional supplies had to be purchased privately). But Julian Holland, whose editorship did not have an easy start, with old hands on the staff resenting his new standards of editorial excellence, opted for a quick route to popularity. He increased the whisky supply to a bottle per shift. Staff in other parts of the radio news empire soon cottoned on. One producer from the *World at One* would routinely head upstairs to *Today* as soon as the programme had gone off air and return to his own office suitably fortified – but not always leaving enough Johnny Walker to keep the *Today* team happy. Editorial standards were not noticeably enhanced when the day shift decided that they too should enjoy a quick morale-booster before starting work.

Nowadays, however, bananas appear to be the essential ingredient of *Today* presentation. Sue MacGregor insists on them too. 'I eat my banana at about five o' clock and, during business [6.15–6.25], we go out of the studio and I have a bowl of Fruit and Fibre. It's always got to be Fruit and Fibre. That routine is something that secures me for all the unexpected things that happen from then on.' Colleagues confirm MacGregor's commitment to the right sort of breakfast cereal. One recalls with wry amusement an e-mail the presenter sent to colleagues just days before the Real IRA bomb blast in front of Television Centre, expressing the opinion that the BBC canteen breakfast trays were 'terrible' – 'nobody eats Weetabix or Crunchy Nut Cornflakes' – and pleading, 'please could somebody put a bomb under those responsible'. 'Does Sue have contacts we don't know about?' wonders her anonymous colleague. 'It was only forty-eight hours later…'.

But even the best efforts of the *Today* presenters to put out a seamlessly professional programme every morning can be thoroughly frustrated by other members of the BBC staff. There is a certain breed of auxiliary personnel, for example, who appear to have no idea what those funny soundproof rooms with microphones are used for. Most reviled are the enforcers of increasingly onerous rules on health and safety. One Saturday morning at BBC Television Centre, for example, John Humphrys had just interviewed a British inventor who had designed an ingenious alternative to the traditional fire-sprinkler system, aimed at preventing the huge costs incurred every time a sprinkler system is activated, by using a myriad of match head-sized sensors, each producing a fine mist of flame-suppressant spray. To demonstrate his technology the inventor set off one of his sensors.

During the recorded item that followed, the jobsworth from Health and Safety barged in. 'You must leave immediately!' he declared. 'A chemical device has been employed in this studio. Do you know what it contained? Do you know whether it was poisonous? You do not! So, until we have identified the precise chemical composition of the device deployed and the exact contents of the spray it produced, this studio is out of bounds. Urine samples will be required from both the presenters present when this device was set off.' John Humphrys offered to provide one on the spot. Colleagues were not sure whether he intended to use a receptacle.

Then there was the priceless moment when a producer rushed into the studio during a news bulletin intending to hand a revised script to one of the presenters – and instead lost his footing and fell, hitting the newsreader hard on the back of the head. Listeners heard a series of disembodied bumps and a brief interruption to the news. One high-profile victim of a *Today* gaffe was the veteran Labour MP Tony Benn, once a BBC producer himself and legendary among journalists for making careful checks to ensure that he is not misrepresented, with whom the programme had recorded a brief interview. Somehow the studio manager managed to play the wrong recording. From radio sets all over Britain came the exotic tones of a Mongolian throat singer.

Other aspects of Sue MacGregor's pre-*Today* routine can also cause surprises in the *Today* office. 'I'm incapable of original thought at three o'clock in the morning when the alarm goes off,' she admits. 'I can't think of wardrobe at that hour. So I actually lay out my clothes the night before – they often turn out to be inappropriate if it's an overly hot or cold day.' I remember the amused fascination among colleagues when Sue turned up for work in a pair of very tight leather trousers.

No matter what is thought by the charmed circle within Television Centre, *Today* listeners have huge regard for MacGregor. She is a less confrontational interviewer than her male colleagues. She has not been the subject of political attack in the way that Brian Redhead, John Humphrys and Jim Naughtie have been. But some admirers argue that, by not generating hostility, Mac-Gregor has allowed the BBC to undervalue her contribution.

The presenter herself is careful not to sound bitter. She is, without doubt, the most high-profile woman on British radio, what one *Today* listener, Katherine Robinson, described in an e-mail to the programme as 'a figure of inspiration for women in journalism'. But MacGregor acknowledges that she is not treated in quite the same way as the male presenters. She is certain there is unfairness and sexism in the way that 'if there is a major political interview on the programme, it will not go to me. It will go to John or Jim. I've given up being cross or bitter about it.'

The important question is whether the BBC's perception of what listeners want from an interview is actually what listeners want. John Humphrys and Jim Naughtie are both masters of the robustly controversial approach. Political hostility is part of the job Humphrys loves: 'The nature of the job insists that sooner or later you're going to upset people. If you're pushing politicians hard enough you're going to be attacked for it.' He is famous for repeatedly interrupting the former Conservative Chancellor of the Exchequer, Ken Clarke (although Clarke himself did not complain and subsequently had the good grace to take part in a spoof interview to mark the 40th anniversary of *Today* in which he interviewed, and interrupted, Humphrys). The disgraced former minister Jonathan Aitken notoriously accused Humphrys of 'poisoning the well of democratic debate'. The presenter has been criticized by Labour politicians as well as Conservatives, notably after a robust interview with Labour's then Social Security Secretary, Harriet Harman, about benefit cuts for lone parents broadcast on *Today* in December 1997, which made her sound vacillating, ill-informed and vague.

Critics of Sue MacGregor, and they include at least one former *Today* editor, say that she has to work hard because she does not have John Humphrys' or Jim Naughtie's grasp of the *Today* agenda. That is a lazy analysis. Certainly she is not a political junkie or former lobby correspondent. On the contrary, her great virtue is that she is not obsessed with the minutiae of the political process and believes that the programme has too often appeared turgidly fixated with arguments and details which have little relevance to an audience beyond Westminster. 'When I do get political interviews,' she argues, 'I hope I get as effective a result as the others. It may not be the sort of Hezza/Humphrys knockabout stuff, or Jim-and-Kinnock kebabbing – but perhaps light is sometimes as effective as heat.' One contributor to an on-line discussion with Sue MacGregor noticed that the smooth relaxation of her voice is even more pronounced when she is asking politicians the toughest questions. 'That's why *Today* has got such a brilliant formula,' says the presenter. 'Because it does tend to marry one kind of presenter with another kind of presenter. I tend to go for elucidation rather than to make a clever political point. I do think that's my role. To pin them down on behalf of people out there who are not other journalists.'

Sue MacGregor plans to leave *Today*, it is understood, in March 2002 on her sixtieth birthday. But she has not yet confirmed that date and it is, she insists, a decision the BBC is happy to let her make herself. But one of *Today*'s most popular and experienced figures will not be presenting the programme for very much longer, and the hunt is on to find a replacement. She must be female.

Today matters so much to the BBC that the choice of presenter is one in which whole tiers of senior management believe they are entitled to a vote. The blundering and cruelty that has characterized the current search show how foolish that corporate attitude is. Winifred Robinson, an experienced *Today* reporter, was carefully groomed as MacGregor's replacement. Colleagues say she was led to believe that the job would be hers after she presented several editions of the programme with smooth professionalism and confidence. But corporate dithering intervened.

Robinson may never know precisely why she was not deemed suitable. One explanation, carefully planted in the *Guardian* newspaper, suggested that her accent – what the *Guardian* called 'a strong lilt of Merseyside' – was the problem. In a leader column entitled 'Accentuate the positive', published on 19 February 2001, the newspaper argued that this was a good thing. 'Too often,' it said, 'the voices of southern England dominate', and concluded, 'if our flagship news programme were to break that habit it would be a cause for celebration, not a fate to be avoided'. Suspecting that Winifred Robinson was to be usurped by Sarah Montague, someone blessed with perfect Received Pronunciation, the *Guardian* accused the BBC's 'powers that be' of paranoid fear that *Today* 'listeners will rebel at being woken by a trio of non-southern accents – John Humphrys' Welsh, Jim Naughtie's Scottish and Ms Robinson's Scouse. So they plan some affirmative action for the English south by opting for a broadcaster born in Guernsey and educated in Bristol.'

There is undoubtedly an unwritten rule at *Today* that, while two male presenters may appear simultaneously (and routinely do), two female presenters is a combination to be avoided. Great fuss was made in the late 1980s when Sue MacGregor and Anna Ford co-presented for the first time, but Sarah Montague, who has since become a semi-regular presenter of *Today*, says that before she first presented the show, she had a conversation with someone relatively senior in management who said, 'It's unlikely we'll put you on with another female presenter because our focus groups show that the public just switch off if they hear two female voices.'

When John Humphrys finally retires, it seems likely that Allan Little will become Jim Naughtie's permanent colleague in the *Today* team, though the other possibility is that the role might go to *Today*'s other regular stand-in presenter, Edward Stourton, who had spent his entire career in television for the BBC and ITN until he found himself no longer presenting the *One O' Clock News* following the notorious reshuffle of BBC television newsreaders. But, while staff at *Today* make it clear that Edward Stourton is a good interviewer, solid, reliable and charming to work with, the BBC has defended him against the *Sunday Express* accusation that he sounds 'too posh'. Little is the more experienced radio broadcaster and has the talent to make a lasting impression on the public. In the spring of 2001 Stourton signed a contact to present *Today* fifty times in the next twelve months. That put him ten shows behind Allan Little's commitment but still in the running.

The BBC's drawn out debate about who to select as replacements for Humphrys and MacGregor is not just about individuals. *Today* is so influential, and presenting it so prestigious, that the Corporation could have almost anyone it wanted. The bigger issue is one of philosophy. What sort of presenter will appeal to the *Today* audience of the future? Should they be younger than their predecessors? Does experience of television guarantee a degree of recognition that was not necessary when Jack de Manio, John Timpson and Brian Redhead were in their prime?

Such questions raise the issue of what career profile makes the best sort of *Today* presenter. Timpson and Redhead were both veteran newspapermen who came to radio without any previous flirtation with television journalism. James Naughtie has a similar background as a senior political journalist. John Humphrys followed a different track, working for the BBC as a television reporter and foreign correspondent, as did Allan Little from BBC local radio to a *Today* reporter and then more than a decade 'on the road' in Eastern Europe, the Middle East, Russia, Rwanda and South Africa. Sue MacGregor, on the other hand, is a classic 'radio girl'.

Do these *Today* stars have common characteristics? Most important are an outsider's combination of interest in and distance from the political and social elites they are called upon to interrogate, and a vast area of what Denis Healey called hinterland. John Humphrys' enormous standing in political and diplomatic circles is that of a privileged and informed observer, not a participant. Brian Redhead, in his very distinctive way, had a similar capacity to probe and analyze without ever becoming part of the agenda he covered. A classic product of the old Scottish belief that the 'lad o' pairts' could succeed no matter how humble his origins, Allan Little has climbed to the top on the basis of ability alone. The young Scot from Dunragit in Ayrshire has no establishment sponsors or friends and no great trust for those who admire status, wealth or power.

I think it is this which makes a great presenter, and it is harder to sustain for a *Today* regular than for almost any other, since the programme's prestige can easily fuel delusions of grandeur in those who present it. As Peter Hobday recalls, six years after he was summarily, and none too politely, dismissed by *Today*, it is the programme which gives the presenter prestige, not vice versa.

The Magic of Radio

It is 6.04 a.m. In Belgrade NATO bombs have started to fall on Serb military and government targets. The *Today* programme's foreign correspondent in the Yugoslav capital has been awake all night. He has seen the flashes in the night sky and heard the explosions that followed. He has ventured out of his hotel to inspect the damage and spoken to frightened, angry, resentful Serbs. He has taken risks to do his job and he has a dramatic story to tell. Your interest in that story is on hold. Your adrenaline is pumping for a different reason. In one minute from now Sue MacGregor is expecting to speak to 'our correspondent in Belgrade'. There is just one problem: he is not there. He's on the roof of the Hyatt Hotel in New Belgrade, but nothing the technical wizards in 'traffic' can do has managed to achieve a connection to his satellite telephone. There is no point in having a correspondent in the thick of the action if you cannot put him in touch with his audience.

Already connected to the studio you have the other half of the story. The BBC news correspondent in Pristina has established a fuzzy line to television centre and is ready to describe the bitter combination of joy and terror experienced by Kosovo Albanians. The item was commissioned as a discussion – Belgrade Serbian opinion talks to Kosovo Albanian opinion via the intermediary of the *Today* programme. Now the correspondent in Pristina is giving you grief. No, she can't wait ten minutes while you try to raise Mike Williams on the hotel phone. She has commitments to World Service radio, Five Live and Breakfast News.

The duty editor leans close to you and says, 'Is he there? I need to know now.' You wait. The duty editor does not – he instructs the studio manager to line up a recorded feature to run as a filler. 'Jim,' he says, speaking into James Naughtie's head-phones, 'have the cue to number 44 standing by. That's number 44, the Faslane package, we don't have Mike Williams yet.' Naughtie nods gently and arranges the papers in front of him. 'Sue,' the duty editor tells Sue MacGregor, 'we don't have Mike in Belgrade yet. We'll have to go with Pristina and I'll bring Mike in if we get him.' MacGregor nods and smiles. There are fifteen seconds remaining before the end of the news bulletin. *Today* is perilously close to kicking off with a whimper rather than a bang.

Then a disembodied voice on the studio tannoy brings joy to your heart. 'Studio 4A, I have Mike Williams in Belgrade for the *Today* programme,' announces the traffic engineer in the base-ment floors below you. 'That's Mike Williams in Belgrade on line three for the *Today* programme.' You lean close to the micro-phone mounted on a console in front of you, depress a toggle switch on the desk and whisper to Sue MacGregor, 'We have Mike Williams in Belgrade. Go to item 5, Balkans Discussion. Belgrade and Pristina are both up.'

The above is a composite. No such precise sequence of events took place. But mornings often start like that when you are the studio producer, the vital link between journalism and technol-ogy. Your job is to make sure that the programme gets broadcast. You need a lot of information at your fingertips. Where are con-tributors and guests sleeping and how can they be reached? Which studios, ISDN lines, satellite telephones or digital mobiles will they be using to speak to *Today*? Do they know how to use the equipment they will be confronted with or do they need technical assistance? Who at dozens of assorted BBC local radio stations is going to take responsibility for ensuring that your guest reaches the contributions studio and makes contact with London? Is that person diligent and helpful, or a resentful member of the local radio old-guard who is much more inter-ested in making sure his own breakfast show gets transmitted than in helping the bloody *Today* programme?

Is one of your contributors depending on his own ability to use one of the BBC's notorious networks of self-operating stu-dios? These are designed to offer convenience, a way of speaking to the nation from tiny towns and villages throughout the UK.

More often they cause chaos. One of the most eccentric and unreliable used to sit in a room no bigger than a broom cupboard behind a small shop in the Scottish Borders. It was created to serve the now defunct BBC Radio Tweed, but soon became a home from home for the Liberal Democrat politician Alan Beith, who could reach it by a short taxi ride across the border from his Northumberland constituency.

Mr Beith regarded the cupboard as a luxury, a good excuse not to travel too far in the hours before dawn. *Today* staff saw it as a technical disaster waiting to happen. For the MP's voice to travel from the 'self-op' to London, a complicated sequence of switches had to be moved in Selkirk by a Radio Scotland employee with no great technical expertise and forty other things to worry about. Before that, a key had to be obtained from a volunteer who also had newspapers and milk to deliver. Even if it worked, Beith had to follow a set of byzantine instructions printed on an apparently pre-war console and then persuade an engineer in London that he really was who he said he was and where he claimed to be. That it worked one time in two was astonishing. Mr Beith never realized how often he was not invited to contribute because experienced *Today* staff could not bear the unpredictability of the 'Borders broom cupboard'.

Studio producers reacted to the place like a kitten to water. It was another element of unpredictability in an already complicated life.

Got all that? Fine. Then you need to know the precise length of every recorded item in the programme and the scheduled allocation of time for each live interview. You need several emergency short versions of the recorded items because some of the live items will certainly run over – either because the editor orders that they should or because the presenter ignores instructions and keeps talking beyond the allocated 'out time'. Seven seconds may once have struck you as an irrelevant, inconsequential period of time, hardly worth worrying about, but if your programme reaches 8.00 a.m. seven seconds late, it won't sound inconsequential. It will sound like the biggest cock-up ever. Imagine it: the pips beeping their familiar greeting to the nation, millions of listeners earnestly anticipating a news bulletin and instead you have a Radio Four trail still bleating on about

Woman's Hour. It hardly ever happens – but it easily could. All it takes is for you to make a mistake.

You didn't want to do this. You are a journalist not a technician. You went into this business to devise original story ideas and treatments – to break news not to cut tape and count syllables. Tough. *Today* is relying on you. All those tricky little fixed points – the sport, the weather, the business bulletin, 'Thought for the Day', the newspaper reviews – they all have to take place at precisely the same time every morning. *Today* staff refer to them as the programme furniture. The creative bits have to be fitted between them. The studio producer's job is to make sure they fit seamlessly.

There is an easy way to do that. Other radio programmes do it all the time. The easy way is to pre-record every interview and edit it to length. That way everything will fit perfectly and the presenters just need to read introductions and relax. But *Today* never works that way. Live interviews give the programme pace and flexibility. They mean the running order can be changed at a second's notice, with breaking news replacing a pre-planned feature or interview. *Today* is relentlessly and deliberately live. Easy options are out.

Studio-producing *Today* is always tricky. The more ambitious the duty editor in the studio beside you, the more demanding it becomes. An ambitious editor cares about journalism alone. He needs a good studio producer to get his ideas on air but he demands maximum flexibility. If a politician reveals something unexpected three minutes into an interview scheduled to last three and a half minutes, the editor will extend the interview. He will speak into the earpiece of the presenter conducting it and issue instructions for a new line of questioning. The interview will continue until the editor is satisfied. Meanwhile, time is ticking by. The next item was due to be a recorded feature. It was four minutes long with a thirty-second introduction to be read by the presenter. If the live interview had stopped at 7.22 a.m. then the feature and introduction would have taken you to precisely half a minute past 7.26 a.m., which would have given time for a live three-and-a-half minute sports bulletin and the news summary bang on time at 7.30 a.m. But now the live interview has filled an additional three minutes and you are stuck betwixt and between. The shortest short version of your feature is too long for the minute and a half you have available – but you can't have 7.30 a.m. at 7.28 a.m.

Solution? Drop the feature and ask the presenters to fill with pseudo-spontaneous banter before and after the sports bulletin – Garry Richardson, *Today*'s regular sports presenter, can be relied upon to help. But less than thirty minutes ago the editor trailed that feature as one of the items 'coming up'. Some listeners will be waiting for it, perhaps even delaying their departure for work or making sure they stay in the car until they've heard it. If it is going to find a slot in the next half-hour of the programme, something else is going to have to give. But that's the editor's decision. Your role is to tell him that his proposed running order won't work.

Live guests are the hardest. They've been tracked down, booked, relentlessly pumped for information to include in the presenter's briefing notes – in many cases they have risen before dawn to take a taxi ride to the nearest local radio station, and unless they are hardened veterans, they are probably excited about the prospect of appearing on the nation's most powerful breakfast show. And then the editor decides he's going to drop them. The voice from 'traffic' speaks to you again. 'Stoke on Trent going through to 4A for *Today*. Stoke on Trent on line four for *Today*.' This time it is not a welcome sound. You know who is in the Stoke on Trent studio. It is an enthusiastic, hard-working local teacher who has introduced a dynamic new syllabus for the teaching of Latin to teenagers. The programme team spotted the idea in a local newspaper and decided it was worth a few minutes.

That was until the political interview ran over. You can't drop 'Thought for the Day' – though like every other member of the *Today* team, you would dearly love to. The newspaper reviews are sacrosanct too, but if asked nicely, the helpful people in the radio newsroom who write them can always shorten them by thirty seconds. The editor's decision is made. The teacher will have to be the victim. 'Drop the classics babe.' (Language can be a little informal in the studio cubicle.)

You call a reporter through from the *Today* office and ask a favour: 'Record an interview with her in the back-up studio. We might just squeeze a few moments on at the tail of the pro-gramme.' You know you won't. So does the reporter. The editor hasn't even been consulted. Everyone except the teacher knows what is going on. She is being mollified by the pretence of a recorded interview with a *Today* reporter. It will not appear on air, although there is a remote possibility that it could turn up as an element in a reporter package. At least she will leave the Stoke on Trent studio without kicking up a huge fuss. It is cruel, and the *Today* programme does it several times per week.

While you were sorting that out, the editor has decided what he wants to run and in what order. You have to calculate permit-ted durations for each of the items – work out whether any of the available versions of the trailed feature can be made to fit the available slot. On a lively morning it is like knitting with hand-fuls of wet spaghetti or tying your shoe-laces with one hand while brushing your teeth with the other. Presenters often describe live radio and television programmes as swans or ducks – elegant and controlled on the surface while paddling frantically beneath the water. What they rarely say is that the frantic paddling is done by the studio producer. If it is done well, the presenters will only know it has happened because the running order on the computer screen in front of them changes. They will not detect any panic or dismay. As studio producer, it is your job to ensure that they don't. Presenters are expensive, fragile, ego-driven beasts. They are also very talented. Good studio producers ensure that fragility is not what comes across to listeners.

When *Today* was based in its original home at Broadcasting House in central London (a base to which it will soon return), senior political guests had a particularly galling trick. Ken Clarke excelled at it. They would delay arrival for the 8.10 a.m. slot until the very last second – sometimes only entering the studio as the presenter read the introduction to their appearance. The tactic was entirely deliberate. Urgent calls to their press officers' mobile phones would elicit reassurance that 'The Chancellor/ Foreign Secretary/Secretary of State will definitely be there in time.' Often they were standing four floors below in the Broad-casting House reception area or relaxing in their official cars just outside the door. Their assumption was that by causing concern in the studio they would put the presenter and the editor on the back foot. They play the same trick now that *Today* is temporarily exiled to Television Centre in West London. Ministers go into the BBC's political headquarters at Millbank to be interviewed – but they still hang about outside until the last moment. It is the studio producer who suffers – snarling gently to him or herself while smoothly reassuring presenter and editor that the key interviewee will be in front of a microphone to hear the first question.

Studio production appeals to certain types of mind. The most creative, lateral thinking journalists are rarely good at it. It requires attention to detail, a longing to create order out of chaos. The way the *Today* programme rota works is something that most team members learn to do at some point in their careers.

Today is a twenty-four hour operation, six days a week. Each edition begins its gestation process just minutes after its predecessor has gone off air. The day team (consisting of a day editor, three producers, a researcher, the forward planning editor, several dedicated reporters and usually the programme editor and his deputy) gather in the programme's 'green room'. The rules are unspoken but clearly understood. The day editor will chair the meeting even though the programme editor is present. Everyone is assumed to have listened to that morning's programme and to have familiarized themselves with the contents of the day's newspapers and news magazines. This is a forum for creative thinking, not an administrative session. Only the naive, the foolish and the doomed turn up at a *Today* programme editorial conference without ideas.

The contents of the BBC's daily 'news prospects' list is discussed. The intention is to identify creative strategies for interpreting, analyzing and clarifying the next morning's top stories. Implicit in this approach is that the *Today* team can make accurate assessments of what those are likely to be.

Today does much more than simply reveal facts. If the school league tables are to be published on a midnight embargo, the bare facts – which schools are top and bottom, which types of school are performing best, etc. – will appear in a bulletin piece written and recorded by one of the BBC's education correspondents. *Today*'s job is to give added value. The editorial conference will discuss how. Should reporters be sent to the best and worst performing schools. Would a debate between the best and worst performing head teachers be illuminating? Will the schools allow reporters access to senior pupils? Would a debate about the benefits and disadvantages of selective schooling be useful?

On a significant story likely to be of interest to a large proportion of the *Today* audience, more than one item will be prepared. School performance is just such an issue. But the programme agenda must be balanced. If there is to be a big domestic story then the international agenda must not be ignored. Politics and foreign affairs are like dual spines running through the collective psyche of the *Today* team. But there is room for whimsy too – for the sort of item designed primarily to amuse and entertain. These are often the items regular listeners appreciate most. Are cormorants beautiful and worthy of protection or vicious predators ruthlessly dedicated to the ruination of recreational fishing? Has there been an explosion in the ladybird population of Britain? (Both items have been discussed on *Today*, both provoked a huge audience response.)

And this is radio. Much discussion centres on how best to bring ideas to air in an immediately accessible manner. There are assorted options – reporter 'packages' (recorded reports containing more than one voice, sound effects and script) can be very economical with time. A skilled reporter can tell a complex story and consider several different views about it in less than four minutes. But there can not be too many packages in any edition of *Today*. Listeners expect to hear the presenters – they trust and admire them – and four minutes of recorded material is four minutes in which the presenters will be idle. Interviews and debates make best use of the presenter team, but only if the right guests are booked – a key part of the day editor's job. If he concludes that a debate about selective education will make a good item for the vital 7.30 a.m. slot, one of his producers will spend the day identifying the best participants. It is not always easy – those who write provocatively on a subject may turn out to be worse than useless as broadcasters. The most lucid exponents of a case can sometimes be economical with the facts. Booking two guests capable of providing a stimulating, coherent and informative discussion – and doing it in less than seven minutes of airtime – can involve speaking to twenty possible candidates.

The morning conference has one overriding objective – to generate sufficient original ideas to fill the next morning's programme. The night editor may throw half of those ideas out before midnight. He may re-arrange the order in which they appear on air. But he has to have the building bricks with which to work. There is nothing more exciting than a night shift during which the world changes significantly. But that doesn't happen very often. An ordinary edition of *Today* is heavily dependent on the ideas generated at the morning conference and those provided by the small forward-planning team which co-ordinates big interview bids (foreign leaders, big-name actors and actresses, authors, etc.) and commissions items in advance to cover predictable set-piece events like conferences, summits and reports by influential think tanks.

The day editor leads the team between 9.00 a.m. and 9.00 p.m. Their work is summarized in a document called 'the prospects'. This is a list of items set up during the day, guests booked, reporter packages recorded, ideas which were attempted but did not work, interviewees who would have been right for the programme but refused to appear. It can stretch to well over a dozen pages of A4 and must contain everything the night editor might conceivably need, from the taxi booking references for the presenters through to contact details for a *Today* reporter on assignment in Kosovo.

Once the prospects are written, a formal hand-over meeting takes place between the night and day teams. From then on the night editor is in charge. His (or hers) is the most exciting job in British journalism and probably the most fraught. He must familiarize himself with every significant news event that has occurred in the previous twelve hours – while he has been sleeping. He must listen to the reports submitted by the *Today* reporters, read the interview briefs, ensure that scripts are written for every item on the programme, react to news which breaks overnight (not least in the newspapers which he will receive by fax and courier from about 10.00 p.m. onwards). Then he must choose which items to broadcast, in which order, allocate each item to the appropriate presenter and ensure that all of this information is entered into the BBC computer system. Night editors need to understand the outer limits of what is technically possible.

But who is this person called the 'night editor'? Journalists familiar with the operation of daily newspapers will assume they know. But while *Today*, and the BBC in general, borrow titles from the older world of print journalism, the job descriptions are fundamentally different. The night editor on the *Today* programme is not one person. He or she can be any one of half a dozen figures ranging from the programme editor, Rod Liddle or his deputy, all the way through to a particularly impressive and ambitious junior producer (or 'Broadcast Journalist' as the BBC officially calls them). And while the night editor on a newspaper is there to make modest late changes to an already complete product, the night editor at *Today* is all-powerful. It is entirely possible that if a *Today* night editor went quietly but entirely mad between the hours of midnight and 6.00 a.m., Britain could awake to several minutes of completely fictitious news or blatant propaganda.

The night editor decides which items will run in each edition of the programme. He compiles the running order and decides which presenter will conduct which interview. He writes the presenters' scripts and approves any amendments they make when they arrive between 3.45 and 4.15 in the morning. He controls the deployment of today reporters and liases with all other departments of the BBC to establish the availability of foreign and domestic correspondents. To listeners accustomed to regarding John Humphrys, Jim Naughtie, Sue MacGregor, Edward Stourton, Allan Little and Sarah Montague as the key figures on the *Today* programme, it may come as some surprise to realize that these excellent and highly paid presenters have almost no say in the content or agenda of the show. They rarely know what will be on the programme when they arrive to present it. No more did Brian Redhead and John Timpson. Presenters do what they are instructed to do by a night editor who will be lucky to earn even a third of what they make.

Night work creates a special kind of bonding. On quiet shifts

Today teams have hours to indulge in the most intimate conversations. Sometimes these move beyond talk. When the programme was based at Broadcasting House, the main office was on the opposite side of the corridor from a suite used by *The World Tonight*. *World Tonight* staff always left the building at 11.00 p.m. They rarely locked the door. In the small hours, while running orders were being written and very little was happening in the world, clandestine *Today* programme couples would have sex in the *World Tonight* editor's office. One reporter, now a widely admired foreign correspondent, treated the place as a private boudoir. His fondness for the location and his forceful personality persuaded other couples to seek alternative locations. One adventurous female producer claimed the studio itself made an ideal location for a discreet rendezvous between the hours of 1.00 a.m. and 3.00 a.m. – after that there was a risk of interruption by the technical staff. Another frequented the Radio One reporters' room colloquially known as 'The Cottage'.

Today night editors are not grizzled fifty-year-olds with decades of experience under their belts. They can be as young as their mid to late twenties. It is a huge weight of responsibility – particularly when something unpredictable happens during the hours of darkness – like the fall of the Berlin Wall or the Armenian earthquake.

From some time around 4.00 a.m. onwards the night editor must explain his decisions to the presenters, massage their egos when one feels that the other has been allocated the more interesting items, and instruct his team to pursue interviewees on stories which have emerged since the day team went home. There may be additional complications to contend with. Do any of the reports he has chosen for use include libellous allegations that need to be excised or thoroughly assessed by BBC lawyers? Have the views recorded in reporter packages been overtaken by subsequent events? Did the day team miss an idea that ought to be on the programme?

Although *Today* is exceptionally well staffed by comparison with its regional and independent imitators, the night team is not large. The night editor has his studio producer, two other producers, one reporter and a programme assistant at his disposal. If a big news story breaks, his resources will be stretched. Even when it doesn't, there is plenty for everyone to do. Let's imagine the night shift from hell. There have been hundreds.

It is midnight. Everything is looking remarkably straightforward. The story of the day is obvious. A long-awaited report on allegations of child abuse at local authority children's homes is due for publication the next morning. The day team and their forward-planning colleagues have done well. The BBC's social affairs editor is scheduled to appear live at 6.10 a.m. He has read an advance copy of the report and is well versed on the findings – amongst which is the conclusion that Home Office supervision of the homes is appallingly inadequate. The Home Secretary has agreed to a live interview at 8.10 a.m. A *Today* reporter has spent a week speaking to victims of the abuse. Her report is harrowing but sensitive and entirely acceptable to a breakfast time audience. The chairman of the independent inquiry panel is scheduled for a live interview at 7.10 a.m., the reporter package will be broadcast after the 7.30 a.m. news bulletin, and the Shadow Home Secretary and her Liberal Democrat rival will appear together at 8.30 a.m. The interview briefs are a little thin on detail – but one of the producers on duty can tidy them up and flesh out the weak points.

The domestic news agenda is interesting and the programme is well set to cover it. An interview has been arranged with the visiting Chairman of the Senate Armed Forces Committee (in Britain to meet with colleagues on the Defence Select Committee). If he can be persuaded to expand on criticisms of the European Union's military ambitions, which he made in a recent interview with the *Washington Post*, his interview may well provoke a good domestic political controversy. The presenter's briefing for that is clear.

On top of all this broadsheet news there are the lighter items. A reporter has compiled four minutes around the news that the homes of the former Romanian Dictator, Nicolae Ceausescu, are to be opened as tourist attractions. There is a short report about a new craze for 1940s dance bands and a lively young scientist has agreed to discuss his PhD thesis in which he argues that chocolate should be free on the NHS to women suffering from clinical depression.

And then, just after 1.00 a.m., first wire reports indicate a major earthquake in Los Angeles. Within minutes the story is confirmed and the BBC's Washington Correspondent files news copy that indicates 'a quake reaching 7.6 on the Richter Scale'. Local emergency services are reporting massive damage, civilian panic, all the hallmarks of a grade one emergency.

The child abuse report still matters but is no longer looking like the lead story. Los Angeles is the new focus of attention. As night editor you must make sure *Today* covers this story on the West Coast of the United States as comprehensively as it had planned to cover the domestic agenda. It will not be easy. The BBC's news partners among the US television networks reveal that they are unable to contact their Los Angeles bureaux. Telephone lines are out of action. Mobile phones are not responding. Computer modems do not connect. There is no word from BBC staff in Los Angeles either. Washington reports that correspondents from San Francisco are setting out for the disaster zone in four-wheel drives. They may take eight hours to arrive.

The night reporter is sent into the self-operating recording studio in the *Today* office. He must call every emergency service, radio station and newspaper in the Los Angeles area. Anybody who has witnessed what has happened has become a source of primary information. Producers hand over every contact they have, professional and personal.

It is 2.00 a.m. In two hours time the presenters will arrive expecting a running order and accompanying scripts. You do not have a programme. The tannoy that connects all BBC news programmes to the central newsgathering operation announces that the air above Los Angeles has been declared an exclusion zone. Only emergency services and military aircraft will be permitted to enter. There will be no eyewitness reports from correspondents flying over the disaster in helicopters.

Correspondents across the USA are beginning to file information gleaned from conversations with US Government departments, military sources and local radio reports from stations in Southern California beyond the worst ravages of the disaster. You hear what they have to report on the BBC's incoming news lines (that can be accessed from the computer matrix on your desk and which you can listen to on headphones) but *Today* is not their current priority. The BBC's twenty-four hour news stations, Radio Five Live and BBC News 24, take precedence now. It is acutely frustrating. Scant resources are being targeted at stations with overnight audiences numbered in mere thousands. The millions who will listen to *Today* are still asleep and blissfully unaware of the tragedy. Your job is to tell them everything there is to know as soon as you go on air at 6.00 a.m. Right now you are not quite sure how that will be accomplished.

Competition within the BBC, the exploding panoply of rolling news and on-line sites, has made your job harder than it used to be. You wonder, not for the first time, whether this really makes sense. What do licence payers want? News whenever they want it or a really comprehensive service tailored to times they are available to hear it? Your bosses have made their decision. The public wants both – and you must live with the consequences.

The first encouraging development comes from your reporter in the self-op studio. She has made contact with the captain of a Canadian Frigate steaming up the US coast towards Vancouver. His ship is standing off the Los Angeles Bay Area, waiting to hear what assistance it may be able to provide. The captain describes a scene of utter devastation. He can see no electric light in the whole of greater LA but the coast is illuminated by towers of flame, which he assumes are the result of fractured electricity, gas and oil lines. The sky is buzzing with US military helicopters. You reporter has recorded a ten minute interview with the captain – but he is willing to give an update later from the bridge of his ship. He is steaming closer to the land. By 6.00 a.m. (that's just 10.00 p.m. in LA) he will have a much closer view.

Your reporter is instructed to edit the interview she has recorded for use as a fall back. Meanwhile she must arrange to call the captain again for a live interview with the presenter at 6.10 a.m. Seconds before it is too late, you remember to thank your colleague for her initiative. A colleague asks whether there are any British or American ships in the same area that might be contacted in the same way? The reporter agrees to check. There is a spring in her step.

You have a familiar queasy feeling. Tragic news stories can so easily seem exciting to the journalists responsible for reporting them. You have to remind yourself that there are almost certainly numerous fatalities in Los Angeles, that the adrenaline of finding out and reporting the story is a perverse but necessary reaction to a horrible event. Make a mental note to keep this at the forefront of your mind. Without it the scripts you write and the tone of the programme you put on air may sound offensively enthusiastic. That breakdown of taste and judgement happens all the more easily when you are covering news that has happened thousands of miles from your own office.

Time is ticking by. You call your colleagues in the BBC Radio News Room. Satellite telephone contact has been established with the correspondent in LA. He is uninjured, but very badly shaken. The walls of his apartment block have been severely damaged. The police have ordered complete evacuation. The news editor's judgement is that your man will be fit to work – and wants to. In the meantime correspondents in the Washington office are compiling detailed reports based on briefings from US government officials, the Red Cross, the Governor of California and interviews with inhabitants fleeing Los Angeles on highways south of the city. This material will be filed in time for *Today*. You request a live interview with the correspondent in Los Angeles for broadcast at 7.00 a.m. The news editor is delighted – Five Live want to speak to him at 6.00 a.m. – but quizzical. Why are you prepared to wait an hour? You only pause for a few seconds before telling him about the captain of the Canadian frigate.

Fair exchange is no robbery. The news editor has your recorded interview copied. He will use short clips in bulletins on all BBC national news broadcasts. You agree that Five Live can have the full version for use at 6.30 a.m. in return for agreeing to make the Los Angeles correspondent available at 7.00 a.m. For once the competing outlets may actually help each other. Necessity is a powerful spur to co-operation.

You have work to do. It is nearly 3.00 a.m. The presenters must have a vague running order. They will understand that it cannot be precise. They have experienced mornings like this before. But your producers will be run off their feet once information starts to flow more freely from Los Angeles. Now is the time to make vital decisions about the material you already have.

The child abuse material is surprisingly easy to deal with. Most of the items remain relevant. They will simply be relegated to second item after the news bulletins and summaries, leaving room to lead with the news of the earthquake at every important junction in the programme (6.10, 6.30, 7.10, 7.30, 8.10 and 8.30). A producer will have to check that the Home Secretary can wait until 8.15 a.m. and will explain to his press officer why the allotted slot has been changed. Similarly, the inquiry chairman will slip down to 7.20. Drop the Shadow Home Secretary and the Liberal Democrat to make way for the Chairman of the Senate Armed Forces Committee; opposition parties will get their chance to attack the government on other programmes later in the day.

The start of the programme is pretty obvious. As soon as the news bulletin has been transmitted you will kick off with the live interview with the Canadian frigate captain. Then the scheduled interview with the BBC's social affairs editor on the child abuse inquiry. But already there is a problem. While the frigate captain's eyewitness testimony will be fascinating, he will still be at sea and in no position to describe conditions among the collapsed buildings of LA. The Canadian sailor will paint a picture from afar, you know he will do it eloquently, but *Today* listeners deserve and expect more. You know you have to find an eyewitness in the city. And the obvious option, the BBC correspondent, is committed to appear on Five Live.

You drop into the self-operating studio. Your reporter has already done well to track down the Captain – but can she find another live guest to complement his contribution? She already has. The control tower at LA International Airport has been converted into an emergency control centre, shepherding the flow of military aircraft already bringing emergency relief to the city. In typical US style the Army and Air Force personnel managing the relief effort are accompanied by press officers. Their task is to communicate accurate news about the situation to the outside world. A woman officer in the control tower has promised to be available to give a live update just after 6.00 a.m. The Canadian and his landbased US counterpart will go on air simultaneously. The first half-hour of the programme is looking promising. You already have enough material to provide a competent service. More will arrive as the BBC teams in the USA begin to file. You type a running order into the computer at breakneck speed. It is 3.15 a.m. and Sue MacGregor will be with you soon.

Now the hard part: allocating items to presenters. Your team this morning is Sue MacGregor and John Humphrys. Many *Today* staff are dismissive of Sue. She is not obsessed by politics. Sue asks questions, does not regard it as her job to engage in verbal combat with interviewees. Some see this as a failing, a relic of her earlier career presenting the gentler, more consensual *Woman's Hour*. It might be fairer to say that Sue MacGregor always remembers that she is broadcasting for an audience, not for journalists.

But the sense that she is not as highly regarded as her colleagues, a suspicion confirmed by the revelation that for several years she was paid considerably less than *Today*'s male stars, has had an effect on MacGregor. She is stubborn about her status. Sue MacGregor will count the number of live interviews on a running order within minutes of arriving in the office. If she has been allocated fewer than her co-presenter, she will point it out. She does not ask why, simply makes a straight arithmetical statement. 'There are fifteen lives in this programme and I appear to be doing six of them.' An imbalance like that is not unusual. Duty editors are employed to make hard decisions about who will get the most out of an interviewee. Too often their assumptions about MacGregor are based on prejudice, not evidence.

When interviewees have a story to tell rather than a position to defend Sue is superb at letting them talk, at steering them in the direction of the most revealing answers. You conclude that she should conduct the opening interviews from Los Angeles and question the chairman of the child abuse inquiry. John Humphrys will handle the social affairs editor, the Home Secretary, and the Chairman of the Senate Armed Forces Committee; MacGregor will deal with the academic with the interesting ideas about chocolate. This is not going to be a morning for presenter tantrums. There will be plenty for everyone to do and much of it will emerge after the programme goes on air.

MacGregor settles at her computer screen to write introductions, read briefings and news wires. You and your team must write draft scripts for the presenters to finesse into their own style. There is nothing you can do to hurry the arrival of information from the USA. Correspondents know about programme deadlines. They will do everything they can to ensure that the material they gather is available for *Today* but they are operating in a different climate. The BBC may be Britain's premier provider of news and current affairs. It has no such status in the United States. Briefings in Washington, DC will be scheduled to serve domestic news reports. The people you are relying on will be looking over the shoulders of CNN reporters and sticking their microphones into gaps between those places held by ABC and CBS teams. The process will produce results, but it is not driven by your needs.

You begin to write, sifting news agency wires for detail and colour to include in scripted introductions to interviews and reports from LA, honing the words left by the day team as suggested introductions to the British news items. And just as you are beginning to panic about not having sufficient detail from America, minutes after John Humphrys' taxi has deposited him at Television Centre, the news tannoy comes alive. The US President has given an impromptu news conference in the White House press room and recorded feeds of his every word are already flowing into the BBC. A producer is detailed to listen to every syllable and edit a version for broadcast at 6.30 a.m. The best segments will appear in the news bulletin at 6.00 a.m. – there is no value in repeating them ten minutes later. A correspondent in Washington has compiled a report from eyewitness testimony broadcast on US television networks. The BBC correspondent in San Francisco has located refugees on the highways outside LA. He will be able to interview them live via a satellite telephone link in his car. One of your producers has woken the head scientist at the seismographic institute at Edinburgh University. He is checking his instruments, but already believes that this is one of the most serious earthquakes in recorded memory.

When you walk into the studio at 6.00 a.m. you feel a palpable sense of relief. The chasing of new interviewees and editing of recorded material has devolved to your producers in the office. If they rise to the occasion there will be a celebration breakfast after the show – coffee and fry-ups in the staff canteen.

It used to be even more fun when the programme was based at Broadcasting House in the heart of London's West End. Then *Today* night teams would go for breakfast at the Titchfield Café – on very special occasions there would be salmon and scrambled eggs washed down with champagne.

It will all work. It almost always does. *Today* has the vast resources of BBC news to call upon and a huge pool of experience among its own team. Your nervousness is not really based on the fear that millions of loyal listeners will wake up to silence. The *Today* team is a bit like a historic regiment. It has battle honours including the fall of the Berlin Wall, numerous British general elections, the resignation of Margaret Thatcher, the Gulf War, the Armenian Earthquake, Bosnia, Kosovo, Sierra Leone. You don't want to be the duty editor who fails to make the mark. Your predecessors all felt the same way.

Who Listens to Today

———

T he reporter was slumped over his desk in *Today*'s old home
at Broadcasting House, a polystyrene cup of tepid coffee
and a leathery piece of toast perilously close to his left elbow. It
had been a busy night. The team had been short-staffed after a
producer with flu was sent home to avoid infecting everyone
else. The old-fashioned switch and lamp telephone system was
buzzing frantically. Three times he lifted his unshaven face and
made mute appeals with his eyes. Please would one of the newly
arrived day team answer the bloody calls? They were too busy
reading newspapers and chatting.

Eventually he bowed to circumstance and picked up a phone.
Carefully disguising the clear, precise diction that would have
made his voice recognizable to thousands, he inquired, 'And did
they tell you who they were putting you through to?' The
answer must have been negative because what followed did not
emerge from the pages of any customer care manual or volume
of advice to BBC staff. 'Right,' said the knackered hero, 'I suggest you fuck right off then.' From colleagues standing close
enough to hear the exchange there was a smattering of applause.

At 9.00, when the *Today* programme ends each morning, there
is a flurry of telephone calls to the programme office. Occasionally they are from political spin doctors or lobby groups desperate to 'correct' something somebody said during the programme.
Usually they are not. The media professionals tend to call during
the programme or before it goes on air – afterwards is too late.
The calls that come in after the show are from 'ordinary' listeners, representatives of the millions for whom the programme is
an established part of the daily routine. There is a joke among
newspaper journalists that any reader who bothers to complain
is, by definition, mad. When a letter written in green ink with

additional comments appended in the margins and highlighted with red asterisks arrives in a newsroom, it is held up as hard evidence that the theory is true.

Today gets its fair share of these irritating protests. A typical example would be a vitriolic protest from a middle-aged male infuriated by the views expressed by a political guest. Such protests usually begin with the words 'In the interview with X at Y o' clock this morning you said...'. The 'you' is always accusatory and always wrong. No *Today* reporter or presenter has uttered any of the words being objected to. If they were said at all (and irritable listeners do have an alarming tendency to misquote), they were the opinions of a guest.

This is explained, patiently, to the listener. The more persistent variety is quite determined not to understand the distinction between the BBC's absolute obligation to impartiality and the contributor's equally precious right to state his opinion as passionately and provocatively as he likes. This species of complainer is rarely mollified. He wants an 'immediate correction', he can prove 'beyond question' that the opinion expressed 'is objectively false'. He has long suspected that the programme is staffed by a 'cabal' of 'socialist sympathisers', 'Tory stooges', 'treacherous pro-Europeans', 'xenophobic Europhobes' or 'screeching lesbian-feminists'. He wants a full transcript, ten minutes of uninterrupted airtime to correct the 'ludicrous' impression conveyed by the item, an immediate appointment with the Director General or, as our anonymous night reporter once argued, 'a pre-frontal lobotomy without the benefit of an anaesthetic'.

When the phones were exceptionally busy, Brian Redhead would occasionally answer one of these calls himself. It was great entertainment to hear the star presenter, in his own unique tones, calmly explaining that 'We don't *think* Mr Redhead has lost his marbles and no, he has never expressed any interest in freemasonry, but we will, of course, keep a careful eye out for symptoms.'

Another tactic, cruelly employed by several *Today* veterans, involves adopting a position still more extreme than that advanced by the complaining listener. Thus a caller might protest 'that Jim Naughtie is so right wing he should join the Monday

Club' only to be told, 'Oh, absolutely. It's a bloody disgrace. But if you think he's bad you should meet Sue MacGregor/John Humphrys/Ed Stourton. Reactionary doesn't begin to describe her/him. But what can we do? David Icke is entirely right. The whole corporation is run by a secret society of alien lizards dedicated to the overthrow of democracy.'

It is the worst kind of contact with listeners, liable to encourage contempt and convey the impression that *Today* has an audience of single-issue obsessives and confused geriatrics. Fortunately, it is not the only way *Today* staff make direct contact with the people they are employed to serve. Out and about in the cities, towns, villages and institutions of the United Kingdom, the programme team are accustomed to encountering enthusiastic fans who stop them simply to say, 'I love your programme', 'I never miss it' or 'Have you met John Humphrys/Sue MacGregor/Jim Naughtie?' These people are infinitely more numerous than the sad minority who plague every broadcaster and who regard a rant at a hapless producer as a good substitute for a call to the Samaritans.

The launch in late 2000 of the *Today* website provided an excellent opportunity for this overwhelming majority of sane, rational, enthusiastic licence payers. Indeed, the enthusiasm with which *Today*'s audience e-mail the site suggests a new definition of the great British middle class. Social scientists need search no further for a classification of what it means to be a concerned and active citizen in the primary years of the twenty-first century. It means you listen to the *Today* programme.

Nearly 6 million Britons hear *Today* every week. Very few hear the whole programme, nor do they all listen simultaneously. Peak audience time is between 7.30 and 8.00 on weekday mornings and between 8.00 and 9.00 on Saturdays. At these times between 2 and 2.5 million people are tuned in simultaneously. But *Today*'s reach is greater than those bald figures suggest. Almost 2 million listeners hear the show between 7.00 and 7.30 a.m. There are often more than a million listening before the 7.00 a.m. news bulletin and a regular 2.2 million at 8.10 a.m. Millions 'make an appointment' to hear one of the main news bulletins and two or three of the reports which follow, setting aside half an hour to concentrate on *Today* before they are obliged to start their working day. Listeners are exceptionally loyal: they listen as often as five days a week, with most hearing three or four editions from every six produced. The statistics are such that broadsheet newspaper proprietors would sell their souls to achieve parity. If *Today* was allowed to accept advertising, it could charge mind-boggling rates for airtime. Advertisers would queue up to pay.

The scale and loyalty of the audience is one of the reasons that small things about *Today* matter so much. The regular time checks are a case in point. If a presenter accidentally says 7.00 when it is really 8.00 or, even worse, 8.30 when it is 7.30, breakfasts around Britain are swamped by waves of short-lived panic. Listeners organize their mornings around the show. Thus the end of the 7.00 a.m. news bulletin is time to get out of bed; if one has not shaved before the 7.25 sports report, the children are likely to be late for school; and the second piece of toast must have been consumed before the end of 'Thought for the Day'.

Part of the programme's success is a simple matter of habit. In Britain, as Jenny Abramsky explains, 'radio has a 90 per cent share of viewing and listening in the morning because people simply aren't watching television. It's one of the things that distinguishes us from the way people in North America consume media. Their breakfast television is very, very powerful. Radio here has been consistently powerful in the morning in a way television never has.'

Furthermore, adds Abramsky, *Today* has some of the hallmarks of a great television programme. 'Now, in the age of the zapper, there are television programmes that people make an appointment to view. So, they watch *EastEnders*, they watch *Coronation Street*. A small group of people watch the *South Bank Show*. On radio people tend to switch on a network (as opposed to an individual programme). *Today* is an exception. It is as much an appointment to listen as *EastEnders* is to view. There are certain iconic programmes where people do that. They stand out in a way that brings in an audience that might not have been listening to that network otherwise. *Today* undoubtedly plays that role... by the time people have listened to *Today*, 50 per cent of the people who are going to listen to Radio Four have consumed it at that point. They will listen three times, four times a week.

'Of course,' she concedes, 'there's a kernel of people who do only listen to the *Today* programme: the switch-off at the end of *Today* is far steeper than at the end of other breakfast shows.' That kernel is a mixture of people who are professionally obliged to listen – the editors, politicians, public relations people and senior executives who simply have to know what will dominate the news agenda in the next twenty-four hours – and those who work such hours that a pre-breakfast appointment with *Today* is their only opportunity to hear serious news and current affairs.

Critics and competitors often suggest that *Today* is elitist, that it concerns itself with issues which matter only to a minority, that it is middle-aged, Home Counties oriented and establishment-minded. The facts are at odds with this perception.

In the late 1980s one *Today* editor, Phil Harding, commissioned private research which showed that the single largest group of *Today* listeners were readers of the *Daily Mail*. I remember that the evidence caused modest consternation among colleagues who had assumed they were writing and commissioning for the delectation of readers of the *Daily Telegraph*, *Guardian*, *The Times* and *Independent*. The truth is that *Today* is doing both. *Mail* readers still make up the largest single slice of the audience, predominantly because the *Daily Mail* is such a phenomenally successful newspaper. A slightly higher proportion of broadsheet readers listen but they represent a higher proportion of circulations which are all considerably smaller than that of the *Mail*.

And *Today* is not unlike the *Daily Mail* in its approach to journalism. It is intelligent but not intimidating. The programme is not exclusive in the sense of being snotty, posh or excessively demanding on the intellect. No radio show designed to be heard and understood by a population engaged in the various routines associated with getting up or, in many cases, driving cars in heavy traffic, can afford to be impenetrable. The current programme editor, Rod Liddle, admits that his editorial agenda is 'aimed more at your classic *Daily Telegraph* or *Guardian* type', but he is well aware that, in straight numerical terms, the audience attracted to a morning appointment with John/Sue/Jim, etc. is very attached to the mixture of news, features and opinion assembled by Paul Dacre's relentlessly successful *Mail*. It is as if the BBC has accidentally stumbled on a formula that manages to be intelligent without being stuffy. Phil Harding went to great lengths to convince his staff that *Today* was not intended for an exclusively broadsheet newspaper reading population of university graduates.

Says Sue MacGregor, who understands this well, 'I never think I'm speaking to 4 or 5 million people. That concept is difficult to grasp. So I tend to talk to one or two people out there. Sometimes they're friends. Sometimes they're my alter ego. Sometimes they're male, sometimes female. Sometimes they're quite young. I'm very conscious indeed that I must assume that most people are not London dwellers, are not chattering classes and are not middle class necessarily. So I tend to assume that although they share my interests, they may not share my life style.

'It's something to do with the intimacy of it. It's a companion to you in the early morning. Most people are busy, whether it's in the car or sending the kids to school or showering or jogging in the park. You can take it with you. You want all the news, and you want it reasonably snappily. You also want argument and you want a bit of fun. And I think occasionally we don't have enough fun. You want a sense of banter. There was a lot of that between Redhead and Timpson.'

In January 2001, when MacGregor and her editor Rod Liddle took part in an on-line discussion with *Today* listeners, it was clear that a few were concerned that the programme can sometimes sound too much like a morning briefing for the British establishment. Did Liddle, asked Matthew Slee, 'see *Today* as part of the establishment'? and 'to what extent are your staff from the right schools and universities?'

'When I joined *Today* a long time ago as a junior producer,' Liddle said, 'four people on the programme had been educated at. Eton and 70 per cent were from public school backgrounds. Mercifully, that is no longer the case and our staff come from a pretty diverse range of backgrounds now. That being said, some people still see us as part of the establishment. Fortunately the establishment doesn't. I think we're a lot more challenging and mischievous than we used to be.'

Another listener, Christopher Andreae, complained that 'Westminster is encouraged to express its opinion on just about everything and it jumps at the opportunity.' The editor responded, 'I think *Today* is primarily a political programme and we do see it as part of our job, the task of holding politicians to account.'

This captured *Today*'s dilemma. In order to remain important to an establishment elite of politicians and media-types, the programme must deliver an audience of ordinary voters and newspaper readers (the people the establishment most need to talk to). The interests of the two groups are not identical. According to Rod Liddle, *Today*'s biggest successes in terms of audience response are not political stories. Liddle identified three that stimulated overwhelming interest among listeners: the suggestion that domestic cats might be shot to prevent them killing so many small birds, a survey of British wildlife which invited listeners to reveal which birds and mammals they could see in their gardens or neighbourhoods, and the revelation that the annual census in 2001 will employ a new means of classifying social class.

Roger Mosey, considered within the BBC to be the most overtly political of *Today*'s editors, admits that he eventually reached a similar conclusion. At an editorial conference he casually asked whether colleagues had noticed a surprising number of ladybirds in their gardens. Several had, so the programme broadcast a report investigating the possibility of a ladybird plague/bonanza. The switchboards almost caught fire. Listeners certainly had noticed an unusual number of the little winged bugs and were eager to share possible explanations for the phenomenon.

So, are *Today*'s listeners a huge pool of animal-lovers with deep insecurities about their social status who have a higher than average likelihood of voting in elections? If that is a fair description of the British middle class then it is a fair description of the *Today* listeners too. They are likely to be over forty-five. They are likely to live in the southern half of England. They do care about animal welfare, education, healthcare and class. They tend to be employed. They are likely to regard the programme as a friend they have invited into their home, and thus to have high expectations about what it will say in their presence. Once people have discovered the programme they are exceptionally reluctant to give it up. None of this means that *Today* does not reach beyond the Home Counties or that it deters younger listeners. There is a myth, wildly exaggerated by those who produce imitations on the BBC's regional radio stations for Scotland, Wales and Northern Ireland, that *Today* is not popular in the devolved parts of the United Kingdom. While it is true to say the programme does not dominate listening in these areas to the extent that it does in the English Home Counties, *Today* has fans in every part of Britain.

Edward Stourton tells a story about an occasion in March 2001 when he was filming a television programme at an undertaker's premises in Rotherhithe, East London. Arriving a little early, he decided to go and get breakfast in a local greasy spoon. 'So, I went in and there were John and Jim on the radio. These were manual workers, truckers, and they were all consuming with avid interest. *Today* was on like a Radio One DJ is on in some cafés.'

Everybody associated with the programme can remember a similar experience. Spending a week in Northumberland searching out quirky stories to fill *Today* during the Parliamentary recess, a very old lady took me firmly by the arm at a rural bus stop. 'You work on the Redhead show?' she asked.

'On *Today*. Yes,' I said.

'Do you know how to find it?' She had recently moved into sheltered accommodation and had been given a new radio by her son. Her old set at home, she explained, had been 'fixed to the right place for years' but she had been forced to do without *Today* since moving because she had no idea how to tune her new radio. Two of her friends were keen to listen as well – but the warden had told her Radio Four wasn't available in that part of the country and the 'music and prattle' of the local radio drove them all crazy.

At her tiny flat I tried the long wave signal. It was as clear as a bell. 'That's it,' she said. 'That's the Redhead station.' Five minutes later she returned with a very old man, wheezing terribly as he smoked a filterless Players Navy Cut cigarette and proffered a tube of superglue.

'What's that for?' I asked.

'So you can fix it there, son. Pour a bit of that on the dial and we'll be safe.'

I tried to explain how easy it was to tune, how they might want to listen to other stations as well – and wouldn't her son be cross if I vandalized his present? They were adamant. They wanted to hear 'Redhead and that Welsh bloke in the morning'. Nothing else. As far as they were concerned, I would be rendering the radio far more useful by locking it permanently onto Radio Four long wave. 'Folk think we're thick,' said the old chain smoker. 'But it gives me a good shout every morning, that show. Some of them politicians tell more lies than an insurance salesman.' I did as I was asked.

In 1983 when the programme introduced its first ever slot for listeners' letters, the response revealed more than a modicum of innate conservatism among the faithful. As ever, *Today* was attempting to move with the times and had decided to experiment with a signature tune. For a few weeks the programme team attempted to maintain the fiction that opinion was divided over the topic of this strange, jazzy jingle. So, the first letters slot, broadcast on 14 January, contained this from P. Langley of Gloucestershire:

Twice *Today*, perhaps tomorrow
I hear with ever mounting horror,
between the cheerful chatter mingle
a silly, senseless, pointless jingle.
Please do not offend the ear.
It's only words we want to hear.
So have a word with your producer.
Keep it for Radios One and Two, sir!

The consensus among listeners was neatly summarized by a caller to the production office who asked whether the team was aware that there was someone playing a saxophone in the corridor outside the studio.

The story illustrates a basic truth. *Today* listeners are very slow to embrace change. In that respect they are a perfect microcosm of the wider Radio Four audience, which has repeatedly shown itself to be tenacious in defence of the status quo, at least until any changes have become as familiar as those they were previously accustomed to. But there is one minor difference. *Today* loyalists have an extraordinary eye for detail and a tendency to be pernickety about the most apparently trivial aspects of the show. In the letters received by the team the most heat is generated by controversial issues like interruptions by presenters – but almost as many get hot under the collar about the use of music and sound effects in reports and the need to identify guests at both the beginning and the end of interviews (it is surprising how many listeners complain that, while they were interested by a contribution, they were never sure who they were listening to). This apparent obsessiveness about form rather than content can give the impression that a large number of *Today* listeners are partially deaf and, by deduction, elderly. But Jenny Abramsky's 'appointment to listen' argument is valid. Those who are busy seem to regard the chance to listen for longer as a special treat to be indulged whenever possible.

Another anecdote makes the point. On Grand National Day 2001, *Today* tapped into the national psyche in its own special way. Aware that a huge number of Britons who rarely gamble on anything else would be making their annual visit to a bookmaker, the programme included a special set of Grand National tips. But these were not the usual racing tipsters' guesses. The three people asked were a four-year-old girl, an astrologer and one of the BBC's regular tipsters. Working without consultation they all identified the same horse.

Several hours later I was in the local bookmaker's diligently placing a couple of pounds each way on the *Today* programme tips. Moments later one of my neighbours, a hard working teacher, marched in to place the same bets. 'Don't know if you heard the *Today* programme this morning,' he confided. 'They had a great idea. It's probably just coincidence, but it must be worth a try.' I'm fairly sure several hundred thousand others did what he did. The odds on the horses identified by the eccentric panel shortened dramatically before the off. Unfortunately none of them won it, but in a race that only saw four finishers, Blowing Wind did manage third place – hard proof that *Today* is as trusted in the West End of Glasgow as it is in Downing Street.

The conventional wisdom is that *Today* 'sets the agenda'. What matters is to understand precisely what that means and how the process works. *Today* is simultaneously a trough from which the British media drinks and a lens through which other editorial judgements are refracted and ranked. If *Today* follows and develops a revelation first made in a newspaper, that revelation will be analyzed and dissected by numerous other publications. In journalistic parlance, the story will be 'given legs' because the *Today* programme has deemed it worthy of inclusion. It may not be fair, sometimes it clearly isn't, but it is certainly true.

It was 6.45 on a Saturday morning, just late enough to deflect the most outraged protests about intrusion. I dialled the home number, half hoping he would not answer. The voice that answered was sleepy, irritable and instantly familiar. The Secretary of State was not amused. 'If you insist on pursuing this issue,' he told me, 'I will hold you personally responsible for any damage to my political career.'

If it was intended as a threat, it sounded more like a plea for mercy. The story dominated the front page of a reputable newspaper. It concerned the issue of export licences for ingredients used in the manufacture of chemical weapons to firms trading with Saddam Hussein's Iraq. Subsequent events would prove that this was too controversial to be killed by one ministerial refusal to answer questions on the *Today* programme. But the minister already knew that. He was terse – but he did not hang up. So I ploughed on. The report was in that day's edition of the *Independent*. He was the minister responsible. Would he respond?

Broadcast journalists only rarely telephone ministers at home. That job is routinely delegated to government press officers who assess the nature of the inquiry and, if they think the minister may be willing to comment, contact the politician themselves. The *Today* programme normally abides by that procedure, but there are exceptions. I was pretty certain no government press officer would risk waking a senior cabinet minister on a Saturday morning – particularly not with news the minister did not want to hear. So I did it myself. The Secretary of State was Peter Lilley, then in charge of the Department of Trade and Industry in Margaret Thatcher's third administration. The details of the allegation are history. I recall the events of that morning to illustrate the power of *Today* and the love-hate relationship which exists between the programme and senior politicians of all parties.

I explained that *Today* had every intention of reporting the allegations. Despite his initial petulance, Lilley assessed the options accurately and fast. He knew what successful politicians all understand but rarely admit. When they talk to the *Today* programme they are not just addressing the general public – no matter how many hundreds of thousands are tuned in – they are also aiming their contribution at a tiny power elite of political colleagues, opponents and friends, and still more importantly, the senior journalists on every national newspaper and television news programme.

As soon as he was convinced that the programme would cover the story with or without his contribution, Lilley became sweet and reasonable. Suddenly he was concerned only about which slot he was going to get. He could not be persuaded that the audience would be higher at 8.30 a.m. (it always is on Saturday morning). His colleagues and advisers had indoctrinated him to believe that 8.10 a.m. was the prestige slot. We settled on 8.10 a.m.

This story was not going away. Peter Lilley knew he had a strong case to argue against those who suggested his department had been negligent in its attitude to the exports. His preferred option was that he should not have to make it. Mud sticks. The plain truth that Britain deals with a plethora of export licence applications every year, and that many of the precursor chemicals used in the manufacture of weapons have legitimate uses, would not prevent days of agonized debate. But if that debate had to take place, and the *Today* programme's decision to report the allegations confirmed that it did, Peter Lilley was determined that his perspective would be heard and heard early.

He was cool and professional on air, his tone just sufficiently short of contemptuous to avoid alienating listeners, and he made sure that his version of the truth was included in every subsequent broadcast, news wire and Sunday newspaper. He did not prevent other journalists pursuing the story but he did change their approach. From the initial appearance of outright scandal he turned it into a more informed debate about the difficulty of preventing legitimate British companies selling intrinsically harmless products. He did not deny that those products could be rendered harmful if used in an irresponsible manner – but was that the fault of the manufacturers and the British government or a reflection of Iraqi willingness to lie about their true intentions?

Peter Lilley's interview turned some of the heat away from himself and his department. He ensured that attacks on the government's policy would be restricted to newspapers which were ideologically hostile to it, and began the process of neutralizing the impact of a potentially damaging revelation.

Politicians, civil servants and opinion-formers throughout the country know that *Today* has this power over the national news agenda. For two decades they have regarded the programme as a platform from which to launch policy initiatives and a pulpit from which to deny and deflect criticism. But an argument has become current in broadcasting and political circles: that the *Today* programme is now a dinosaur, a relic of a gentler past which died with the advent of digital television, rolling news channels and the internet.

BBC executives, including the Corporation's head of television news, Roger Mosey (himself a former editor of *Today*), also subscribe to this view. Their opinion is that before the birth of services like Sky News, BBC Radio Five Live and the 24-hour digital channel News 24, the *Today* programme would always obtain the first interview with the most important figure concerned in a story. Now, they say, that is no longer true. Sure, *Today* can still excite interest. It still appeals to the 'Westminster Village' of politicians, lobbyists and political journalists. But it is no longer first with the news. The resignation of Peter Mandelson as Secretary of State for Northern Ireland, Roger Mosey patiently explained to me, was precisely the type of story *Today* would once have made its own. He described with great enthusiasm how Mandelson had decided to give broadcast interviews on the afternoon before his second and final departure from the Cabinet – whereas, in Mosey's view, five or perhaps ten years ago, Mandelson would have kept his powder dry and waited for a key slot on the next morning's edition of *Today*. In the new world of round-the-clock news he appeared on News 24 that afternoon and proceeded to make a tour of television news studios. The story was firmly in the public domain long before *Today* got a chance to cover it.

This is not untrue. But it has had nothing approaching the impact Mosey implies. Indeed, his argument had been disproved before News 24 existed, even before the launch in 1994 of BBC Radio Five Live. There was certainly resentment among staff at Radio Four when the BBC decided to launch a twenty-four hour rolling news station. Traditionalists felt the Corporation was setting up a station to compete with itself. They feared the *Today* programme's audience would be slashed by defections to Five Live and that guests who had once begged to be on the great flagship programme would no longer bother to appear. Other BBC programmes privately hoped this would happen, for *Today*'s popularity among listeners is matched only by the resentment from those on competing news programmes, who consider it too bloody smug by half.

But the collapse of *Today* simply did not happen. Not when Radio Five Live took to the airwaves and certainly not as a consequence of the BBC's stubborn determination to pour millions of pounds into a television news channel very few bother to watch. Nor did the politicians find it as easy as they hoped to pull the rug from under *Today*, though they would no doubt like to. The Prime Minister's press secretary, Alastair Campbell, has made it very clear that he resents the programme's style, tone and influence. He would prefer to present Labour Party policy via less challenging outlets like *GMTV*, *Richard and Judy*, regional television news and populist phone-in shows on BBC and commercial radio. He has tried.

Many Conservatives feel still more hostile towards the show. They distrust the BBC's public sector status and suspect *Today* of harbouring powerful social-democratic instincts. In October 2000 these suspicions were turned into concrete policy. William Hague became the first opposition leader in decades not to appear on *Today* during his party conference. Conservative Central Office insisted this was the result of scheduling problems, not a formal boycott. Rod Liddle, *Today*'s editor, is certain that this is nonsense. Staff in the party's press office told him a conscious decision had been taken to undermine *Today* by not allowing Hague to appear. The Conservative strategy failed as completely as Alastair Campbell's desire to protect Labour ministers from John Humphrys and Jim Naughtie did. Hague returned to *Today* a few months later, all notions of boycotting abandoned.

Quite simply, there are millions of reasons why *Today* has retained an influence – 6 million of them tune in each week. Think of it in terms of your own friends and colleagues. Among them will be readers of every newspaper in Britain. The *Daily Mail, Daily Telegraph, The Times, Guardian, Independent, Daily Express, Financial Times, Herald, Scotsman, Western Mail, Belfast Telegraph, Yorkshire Post.* Some will read the same newspaper every day. Others chop and change, buying particular editions because they enjoy individual columnists or want to scour that day's job advertisements. But the combined sale in the world's most diverse and imaginative newspaper market is not much bigger than the *Today* programme's daily reach.

There is another obvious problem. To read every interesting column, eyewitness news story or leader comment you would have to spend hours scouring all the newspapers. You don't have time and nor do many of the people you know. So you read the bits that interest you from your newspaper of choice and get your sense of what matters from *Today*.

You will have read about politicians' alleged fixation with the editorial stances adopted by individual newspapers. Tony Blair is terrified of the *Daily Mail*, isn't he? Rupert Murdoch and his *Sun* newspaper delivered a Conservative victory against the odds in 1992 ('It was the Sun wot won it'). Certainly politicians care about anything that achieves mass circulation – but they know very well that broadcast news is more influential than newspaper comment, and broadcast news that dominates the morning market is twice as important as programmes that follow later in the day.

The *Today* programme's influence depends on what journalists call critical mass. A story has reached critical mass if so many people are talking about it that it simply cannot be ignored, even by those who would rather it was not being discussed at all. Individual newspapers can bang on and on about an issue for weeks at a time, but if their obsession is not reported by broadcasters, it will take a long time to reach critical mass. If the newspaper is a small circulation broadsheet, it may never do so.

In 2000, for example, the *Guardian* decided to launch a national debate about the future of the monarchy. Adopting a proudly republican stance, the newspaper sought to provoke a nation-wide discussion about whether a modern democracy should retain absurdities like the hereditary principle. The thesis was entirely coherent and the *Guardian*'s writing was bold, incisive and stimulating. But, despite weeks of effort, the *Guardian*'s campaign did not reach critical mass. There was no national debate – simply a private conversation between *Guardian* readers, many of whom agreed with the newspaper's suggestions for modernization and reform of the British constitution. This was not surprising. The editor would have been committing commercial suicide if he had not been confident that his core readership is unenthusiastic about the Windsor family. If the *Today* programme had suggested abolition of the monarchy, there would have been a constitutional crisis by lunchtime.

A painful example from my own direct experience makes the point well. It happened in the year 2000, well after the media explosion that was supposed to kill *Today* as the nation's primary agenda-setter. On 27 August 1999 the *Scotsman* newspaper, where I was then the deputy editor, published a story of which I was, and remain, intensely proud. It revealed that a spy at the heart of NATO's command structure had passed advance details of Alliance bombing raids to the Yugoslav high command in Belgrade during the early weeks of the Kosovo war. Flight plans, known as air tasking orders, had been leaked first to the Russian defence ministry in Moscow and from there to Belgrade. The espionage had lasted for several weeks and had only been stopped when NATO suspicions were aroused by the destruction of a FI17A Stealth Bomber assigned to attack the defence research base at Bujanovci, north-west of Belgrade, on the evening of 28 March 1999.

The story was a vindication of the *Scotsman*'s investment in foreign news reporting and a real feather in the cap of foreign editor Andrew Macleod. The *Scotsman* had first heard about the spy allegation from a freelance contributor, the celebrated defence analyst Paul Beaver. With typical caution Beaver had explained that his sources were excellent but that they would deny the allegation if it was published. I knew that we had to find corroborating evidence. A team of journalists made up of Balkans correspondent Chris Stephen, Brussels correspondent Alexandra Blair, reporter David Montgomery and assistant foreign editor James Kirkup set to work under the guidance of Andrew Macleod and myself. We were helped by the *Scotsman* stringers in Washington and Moscow.

Gradually, from sources in London, Washington, Brussels, Belgrade, Pristina and Moscow we gathered confirmation that the information we had obtained was not carefully planted Yugoslav propaganda. Beaver's original story was accurate. NATO knew that it had been infiltrated. It knew that vital information had been given to the enemy. Urgent steps had been taken to plug the leak as soon as it was discovered. Several of the military and political officials who confirmed our inquiries offered us suggestions about the identity of the spy, but we were persuaded not to identify him by a very senior military source who warned that different NATO members were competing to apportion blame to each other and that the hints at precise identity were politically motivated. The British military were keen to blame the French, some in the US camp pointed the finger at Italy.

The *Scotsman* story was painstakingly researched, checked and checked again. The icing on the cake came in the form of a picture depicting one of the Serbian surface-to-air missile launchers that had participated in the ambush or 'SAM Trap' which downed the Stealth Bomber (the only Stealth ever to be destroyed in combat). This was a genuine world exclusive.

I had just one concern. Between 1997 and 2000 the *Scotsman* had broken a series of exclusive news stories that confounded any impression that it was only agenda-setting on Scottish affairs. We rarely got any credit for them. The British and international media establishment only noticed when they were picked up and published by London-based broadsheets or mentioned on the *Today* programme. I was determined that nobody else should get credit for revealing the existence of the NATO spy. The thoroughness with which Andrew Macleod and his team had tracked and confirmed the story would have been impressive if it had been carried out with all the resources of the *Washington Post*. I used every technique known to journalism to ensure that this exclusive would be widely reported and properly attributed.

I knew first that I had a story that ought to make headlines around the world, and second that it would be denied by NATO. Knowing that sources will lie if challenged is one of the most frustrating things that can happen to a journalist, but I hoped that other newspapers and broadcasters would seize on our allegations and put new sources under intense pressure to confirm our report. To orchestrate that pressure I made sure details of the *Scotsman*'s investigation were made available to news agencies and broadcasters as soon as the first edition of the newspaper began to run off the presses. I made a particular point of briefing the *Today* programme.

As expected, the *Scotsman*'s story was denied by NATO. Alliance spokesmen said we 'had no evidence' and 'could not substantiate' our allegations. The world believed NATO. Even the *Today* programme, which carefully and accurately reported and attributed the *Scotsman*'s exclusive on the morning of 27 August, seemed content to accept assurances that really there was no NATO traitor passing intelligence to Belgrade. The BBC reported speculation that a lucky strike by Serb air defences had been cleverly used to disrupt NATO staff work by 'starting a hunt for an imaginary spy'. It did not feel like a case of credit where it was due, more an example of potential damage limitation – as if the BBC was saying 'Do not be fooled, this is not a BBC report. We are simply bringing it to you second-hand. So if it turns out to be wrong you'll know who to blame.'

And they did know who to blame. In Washington, DC, CNN originally got so excited about the story that I could not get them off the telephone, but then called back to tell me I was wrong. The Pentagon had arranged a special briefing for their defence correspondent: there was no spy and never had been. The story, which had briefly appeared at the top of the CNN running order, was dropped almost before it had appeared. Only *Channel Four News*, an oasis of journalistic courage and impartiality, had the common sense to interview Paul Beaver, who gave a typically impressive account of himself and of our story. That was it.

Several months later the reaction was very different. It was 6.00 on a cold Thursday morning in March. The bed was warm, the children were asleep and I had consumed a lot of wine with dinner. Radio Four was on, as it always is, but I was hardly listening. Bang! Suddenly I was.

The item in the short news bulletin which starts the *Today* programme was brief but enticing. A spy at NATO headquarters had leaked secrets about the Kosovo campaign to the Yugoslav military command. BBC correspondent Allan Little had seen details of a secret US military report. Full details would follow later. I listened to everything Allan Little said and, as soon as he had completed his contribution to *Today*, called the programme office.

'Allan? It's Tim Luckhurst. I love your story about the spy at NATO. In fact, I adore it. It's almost identical to the story the *Scotsman* published last August, and you are giving us no credit at all.'

Allan Little is too good a journalist to deliberately borrow without attribution. He was more concerned than angry. We argued for a while about whether *Today*'s was precisely the same story, and then Allan agreed to see that in the pieces he was doing for the television news at 1.00 and 6.00 the *Scotsman* was credited. That was 9 March 2000. What happened next is the crucial issue.

Little had uncovered his story while researching a television documentary, *Moral Combat: NATO at War*. BBC news had taken what it considered the freshest and most exciting revelation in the documentary and trailed it on the *Today* programme, which ensured it would be heard, followed and repeated by all the mainstream television and radio news programmes and by newspapers too.

By lunchtime a global fencing match was underway between the BBC and NATO. In Brussels the alliance's official spokesman, Jamie Shea, went on the record and insisted there was 'no evidence for the allegations'. *Today*'s defence correspondent Andrew Gilligan included this non-denial in his scripts but added new detail from off-the-record briefings. 'The mole has not been caught,' said Gilligan, 'but heavy hints are being dropped that it was not a leak from NATO headquarters itself, but from one of the national delegations attached to it or from a national government.' It was the old 'blame the French' line which we at the *Scotsman* had dismissed as unreliable without further detailed substantiation.

The BBC was not giving up on the story. *Today* had placed it in the public domain. NATO would have to do better than the weak and ambiguous denials which had got it off the hook when the *Scotsman* published its story. In Ankara, Turkey, the alliance's Secretary General, Lord Robertson, was confronted with a microphone. Challenged to confirm or deny the spy allegation, he employed a more expansive version of Shea's non-denial – that NATO had 'no knowledge and no evidence that air-tasking orders, which allocate missions and targets, were ever passed to the Serbs or otherwise compromised'.

NATO's strategy was to 'close the story down'. Neither Jamie Shea nor Lord Robertson had said the story wasn't true, but they hoped that by saying very little they could take the heat out of the controversy and avoid providing the sound bites and pictures that would help journalists to keep it moving. It wasn't working. In London the Conservative opposition scented an opportunity to embarrass ministers. The media, including the BBC, reported their demand for an official inquiry into 'reports that NATO's bombing of Serbia during the Kosovo war was compromised by a spy at the heart of the western alliance'. And the rest of the world was beginning to pay attention too. 'Pentagon: NATO Kosovo Air War Data Leaked' was the *Washington Post*'s headline on a story by staff reporters Roberto Suro and Thomas E. Ricks. NATO's attempt at non-denial was falling apart, and in London the *Guardian* twisted the knife. Under the headline 'Spy Report Shakes NATO', Richard Norton Taylor, Julian Borger and Ian Black wrote 'NATO last night was forced into an embarrassing climbdown when it admitted that, contrary to earlier denials, a secret US report exists suggesting it had a spy in its ranks in the early days of the Kosovo War... . A definitive "lessons learned from Kosovo" study has been drawn up by James McCarthy, a now retired US air force general, for the deputy secretary of defence John Hamre and general Joe Ralston, vice-chairman of the US joint chiefs of staff [which] says that after NATO reduced the number of people with access to bombing raid orders from 600 to 100, the effect on what the Serbs appeared to know about NATO's plans was immediate.'

The *Today* programme had done the trick – from spectacular allegation to confirmed truth in just twenty-four hours. On the editor's private terrace overlooking Salisbury Crags at the *Scotsman*'s Edinburgh headquarters I paced and smoked resentfully. My foreign editor was furious. The story *Today* had placed on the global agenda was essentially the same story the *Scotsman* had published on 27 August 1999. Having worked for both, I am acutely conscious of the difference in scale between BBC news and the *Scotsman* newspaper, but that wasn't the crucial factor. The *Today* programme was. By trailing Little's documentary in an item on *Today*, the Corporation alerted the British establishment, millions of other listeners and its own programme teams that this was something big and significant.

Today could have promoted and defended the *Scotsman*'s version the previous year, and had it done so, other BBC programmes would have come under pressure to test the validity of NATO denials. But *Today* staff are accustomed to regarding newspaper journalism as a resource from which they can pick and choose. The habit is resented in newspaper circles because *Today* regularly manages to push a story up the national agenda when it has played no role in uncovering or revealing it. As the spy saga illustrates, *Today* can achieve startling results in return for very little work. If several million homes had the *Guardian* or even the *Scotsman* delivered to their doors at public expense (or, better still, read to them over the radio), their influence would be comparable.

The old adage about imitation and flattery is the final element in proving the scale of *Today*'s regular audience. If you are in Scotland, tune one radio set to Radio Scotland's *Good Morning Scotland* programme and another to *Today*. After thirty seconds you'll have noticed that the entire tone and format of *GMS* is a direct copy of *Today*. Listen longer and you'll hear the same reports appearing on *GMS* as on the *Today* programme, but about thirty minutes later. The reason is simple: one of the *GMS* team is recording the *Today* programme in order to rebroadcast its best elements in his own show.

Do the same in Wales or Northern Ireland. The BBC's regional breakfast shows in both places are co-presented facsimiles of the original programme. RTE's *Good Morning Ireland* is another flattering copy. Move to Washington, DC and tune to National Public Radio's *Morning Reports*. Now where did the idea for that come from? A former producer is candid: '*Today* is the benchmark of excellence in news and current affairs radio.'

The Things They Do for Today

———

Conflict and tragedy make for exciting broadcasting. Sad, but true. *Today* has made a name for itself by bringing the news first to millions of breakfast tables. On the morning of 22 December 1988, for example, John Humphrys identified the iconic image that to millions of people in Britain and America still says 'Lockerbie'. After the bombing of Pan Am Flight 103, the presenter had flown to Glasgow late that evening and driven through southern Scotland to be live on the scene of the tragedy when listeners awoke. In his presentation from the crash scene Humphrys focused, in taut, economical prose, on the macabre sight of the aircraft's flight deck. 'Cordoned off by police now,' he reported, 'is a piece of wreckage which looks like a bit of an aeroplane. It's the nose of the huge jet, the cockpit more or less intact. It landed upright and if you let your eyes travel only so far from the cockpit windows, you could believe the rest of the aircraft is still attached to it. Only it isn't. Many bodies have been recovered by now but those of the pilot and his flight crew still sit where they were when their aircraft fell from the sky...'. It was an audio equivalent of the picture that was to grace the front page of hundreds of newspapers just twenty-four hours later.

On 12 October 1984 John Timpson's greeting must have stirred many listeners from partial wakefulness to fully alert in a matter of seconds. It did that for me. 'Good morning from John Timpson in Brighton,' he began, 'where, at ten to three this morning, an explosion extensively damaged the Grand Hotel in which the Prime Minister and a number of her Cabinet were staying.' For many, that was the first they heard of the IRA bomb that came so close to killing Margaret Thatcher and the principal members of the British government.

There are numerous other examples. Barry Norman

announcing the end of the Vietnam War on 5 May 1975. Brian Redhead interviewing reporter Tom Brooke live from the Dakota building in New York just two hours after the death of John Lennon. Sue MacGregor's incisive interview with Sarah Ferguson about the collapse of her marriage to Prince Andrew, which drew out Ferguson's candid confession that 'I do honestly admit to being gullible and naive' about the lifestyle the Royal Family would permit her to have. Or the extraordinary interview in which Diana Bowran, the British nurse who treated a dying President Kennedy, spoke for the first time about how Jackie Kennedy 'wouldn't let go of him. She clung on to him' as JFK was wheeled into the emergency room.

These are what journalists call set-pieces: distinguished professional responses to dramatic events which are there for all to cover. But at its very best *Today* has the money and the personnel to do more. The enviable cushion provided by the much criticized licence fee allows the programme to invest in speculative missions, trips that may produce nothing worth broadcasting but which, when they work, result in journalism that can change government policy by creating national interest. *Today* does not need to make overtly unreasonable demands on staff. Among the young ambitious graduates who fill the entry-level production and reporting roles on the programme, the desire to get noticed is powerful. Usually they will volunteer for risky assignments to bring news that would otherwise not be heard, often because they want to and sometimes because they know a colleague will grab the opportunity if they do not.

Tom Carver, now a BBC news correspondent in Washington, DC, is an example of a *Today* reporter who went well beyond the call of duty to serve the interests of the programme. What he did at the end of the Gulf War illustrates the risks *Today* staff will take and the impact their actions can have.

In 1991 Carver was among several members of the programme staff, including myself, who volunteered to join the BBC news teams dispatched to the Middle East to cover the Gulf War. The Corporation had learned many lessons from the reporting of the Falklands conflict nearly ten years earlier when, it recognized, the British government and military had been exceptionally adept at controlling access to information. This time the BBC was determined to provide 'warts and all' coverage. It went to great lengths to ensure that listeners and viewers got considerably more than the sanitized news released by the Ministry of Defence.

During the war Carver was based in Saudi Arabia. He entered Kuwait with allied ground forces and was flown home after witnessing the liberation of Kuwait City, the terrible destruction on the Basra highway and the miserable lines of Iraqi POWs. Carver believed his war was over, a view confirmed when BBC doctors advised him that his lungs had been polluted by fumes from the burning oil wells set ablaze by retreating Iraqi soldiers.

Returning to the *Today* office in London, Carver was told by the editor, Phil Harding, about 'an awful situation developing in Northern Iraq' – and was surprised to be asked if he would be willing to attempt an assignment to Iraqi Kurdistan. Harding had guessed that Saddam Hussein's renewed persecution of the Kurds would become one of the most controversial consequences of the Gulf War. When he asked Carver to go, he could not have known that the reporter's work would play a vital part in bringing the plight of the Kurds to world attention.

Carver knew the proposed mission was dangerous. He was not at all certain it was possible. There was no direct route to Kurdistan. Access would have to be gained on foot – either from Turkey or Syria. Everyone on the programme knew that, before deciding to become a journalist, Tom had served briefly as an officer in the British Army. It was assumed that he knew how to look after himself and was best left to operate on his own initiative.

Despite feeling extremely ill after his experiences in Kuwait, Carver had no intention of missing the opportunity. Painfully aware of how unprepared he was, Carver also knew how naive his editor was being in assuming he could even get to Kurdistan, let alone file reports if he made it. His first stop was a map shop in London's Covent Garden. There he bought aerial maps prepared by and for the Royal Air Force. He vividly remembers wondering how much use they would be. They showed the topography of the region in great detail but did not include many indications of the existence of towns, villages or roads. The maps were designed for a pilot flying over the area, not as a guide to entry by land.

Noting that the mountains on the Syrian border with Iraq were not as tall as those on the Turkish frontier, he guessed that snow cover would be less of a problem if he entered via Syria. It was the first of several decisions that may well have saved his life. That night Carver met with Nick de la Casa, an agency journalist who was planning a similar mission to Kurdistan. De la Casa had decided to travel via Turkey. Carver was tempted to join him. Several weeks later he was both sickened and relieved when he discovered that Nick de la Casa and his companions had been murdered by the interpreter who led them across the Turkish border.

Carver duly booked a flight to Damascus. It is an indication of the ad hoc nature of his mission, and the relaxed attitude the BBC then had to risk taking, that he had no Syrian visa, no Syrian currency and no absolute certainty that Hafez al Assad's ruthless police state would even let him into the country. Neither the BBC nor the British Government would be able to do anything to help him where he was going.

At Damascus airport his trek nearly ended. Without a valid visa Syrian officials refused him entry. Carver had the telephone number of Louis Faris, the Radio Monte Carlo stringer in Damascus, and a local legend who combined this job with a role as honorary consul of the Philippines, an import–export business of dubious legality and an encyclopaedic knowledge of Syrian officialdom. Carver suspected that if he could telephone Faris, his acquaintance in Syria would know how to arrange a retrospective visa and who to buy it from.

There were just two seemingly insurmountable problems. First, the telephone Carver needed to use was tantalizingly visible on the other side of the customs desk – but without a visa, Syrian officialdom would not let him reach it. Second, Carver had not a cent in Syrian currency. If he did get to the wall-mounted phone, he did not have the coins to make a call. He imagined the silent ridicule of the *Today* programme. Poor Tom. A former soldier, intrepid veteran of the Kuwait campaign, incapable of circumnavigating the most basic bureaucratic hurdles. Next time better to send someone less scatty.

Carver remained calm. Shouting at Syrian security officers is a sure-fire way of causing oneself problems. Please could he use the phone? He wouldn't wander off. He would come straight back behind the customs desk. It would be terribly kind. Eventually they relented. He inserted a British two pence piece.

It worked first time. The semi-legendary (and now dead) Mr Faris, a devotee of evil-tasting synthetic whisky and Cuban cigars, answered almost immediately. Not long afterwards, Carver's saviour arrived surrounded by bodyguards and made all the right payments to all the right people. The journalist was officially admitted to Syria. He remembers the Damascus flat of 'Mr Big' as piled high with contraband and carefully guarded by a collection of deeply menacing men. Louis Faris was obviously deeply entrenched in Syrian society. He knew how to make things happen. After a decent rest and a lot of useful advice, a car and driver were arranged to take Carver to the border with Iraqi Kurdistan.

In the far north-eastern corner of Syria, about as far from Damascus as it is possible to travel without leaving the country, the borders of three nations – Iraq, Turkey and Syria – meet at the source of the river Tigris. The Roman relics that scattered Carver's route were entirely unspoiled by the ravages of tourism. There was no way of telling the *Today* programme where he was. He had no satellite telephone, no laptop computer, none of the technology that would now be standard for a reporter attempting such a mission. Such things did exist in 1991 – but they were much bulkier than they are today, and carrying them would have been a serious encumbrance. Carver was carrying nothing that would not fit in a single rucksack.

His driver placed him in the care of a group of Kurdish KDP (Kurdistan Democratic Party) fighters, implacable foes of Saddam Hussein, who used Syria as a base for cross-border raids into Iraq. True to their tradition of hospitality, the Kurds were delighted to help a BBC reporter. But there would be no hurry. They would take him across the Tigris and guide him into the Kurdish town of Zakho in northern Iraq, but he would have to be patient. Crossings could only be attempted when intelligence indicated that the Iraqi Army was not lying in wait.

After three days and nights, the Kurdish fighters judged it safe to attempt a crossing. Carver was less certain. The moon was full, providing excellent night-vision. Writing about it later,

Carver described it as a 'huge full moon' burning 'like a false sun in the open sky'. If Iraqi soldiers were hidden on the opposite bank, they would surely spot the infiltrators. But the Kurds were determined and Carver resolved to accompany them. The party had been joined by a very overweight American reporter who seemed less than entirely aware of the danger they were facing. It would not do for the *Today* programme to be scooped by American broadcasters. A shallow rowing boat was produced and, despite the dangerously clear and illuminated sky, Carver climbed in. 'Not for the first time in my life,' he said later, 'I carried on because I lacked the courage to go back.'

The KDP and the journalists set off to paddle across the Tigris. The moment is seared on Tom Carver's memory. 'Iraqi artillery began to shell us almost immediately. One shell fell a few yards to the left of our raft. Seconds later another fell to our right. I may never have been the world's best soldier, but I knew enough to understand what bracketing meant. If they land one to the left and one to the right, the next one should come down in the middle.'

But although the Iraqi fire continued relentlessly, the killer shell did not land. Carver and his companions found themselves searching desperately for cover on a shingle beach on the Iraqi bank of the Tigris. Their position was cruelly exposed but they could not move on. The danger of running straight into Iraqi ground troops was too high. They resolved to spend the night on the beach. 'We had only just reached that decision,' Carver remembers, 'when the American reporter pulled a huge, Day-Glo orange sleeping bag from his rucksack. I was horrified and absolutely frantic to stuff it back, or just get rid of it altogether. He might as well have illuminated a neon sign and invited them to shell him to pieces. The guy was completely out of condition and utterly clueless.'

Having got this far, Tom Carver was determined to file for *Today*. If he was going to endure a night under Iraqi artillery fire, there was damn well going to be a point to it. At dawn the next morning the KDP managed to lead Carver, and the injudicious American, off the beach and into the hills. Eventually the *Today* man managed to hitch a lift on a Kurdish farmer's tractor and headed in the direction of Zakho.

Throughout his time in Iraqi Kurdistan, Tom Carver was given hospitality by the combined forces of the two main Kurdish rebel groups, the KDP and the PUK (Patriotic Union of Kurdistan). KDP and PUK forces have fallen out since 1991, and had not always made common cause before then, but this point in March 1991 was a period of euphoria for them. Saddam Hussein had withdrawn large elements of his army from the Kurdish territory in northern Iraq in order to fight the Gulf War and to suppress post-war rebellions by Shiite Muslim fighters in the territories south of Baghdad. Liberation seemed a real possibility and the Kurdish factions had put aside their internecine squabbling to unite in the cause of national liberation. Carver found their hospitality and generosity breathtaking. They had very little food or drink but what they did have was offered to him. He spent several days in the mountains above Zakho recording interviews and commentary for a *Today* programme report.

Then reality dawned again. There were no telephone lines out of Kurdistan. His work was all recorded on a Sony professional cassette recorder. He had no idea how to get it back to London. The Kurds told him to put all of his work on a single cassette tape. One of their fighters would take it back across the Tigris into Syria and ensure that it reached the BBC man in Damascus. Surely he could play it over a telephone line to London? The theory sounded fine but Carver had no real expectation that his work would ever reach *Today*. 'But I didn't have a better idea, so I recorded all the package elements on a cassette tape and the Kurds sent it back to the Tigris by tractor. Three days later I was still sitting above Zakho listening to the BBC World Service on my short-wave receiver. I heard myself reporting from Kurdistan. It was truly amazing. Louis Faris in Damascus had played it over to the BBC on his mutter-box [a crude compressor which slightly enhances the quality of a telephone line and allows reporters to file radio reports via conventional telephones]!'

But the World Service was carrying alarming news too. Iraqi armoured columns were heading north from Baghdad and back into the Kurdish controlled areas. They were close to Zakho and Kurdish refugees were streaming into the mountains by the thousands.

Carver headed down from the mountains into the town of

Dohuk. He arrived there at the same time as Jalal Talabani, the leader of the Patriotic Union of Kurdistan. Joyous crowds swamped the PUK building, Dohuk was experiencing a last moment of freedom from Saddam Hussein. It did not last long. Talabani was forced to pull out less than twenty-four hours after he arrived. His lightly armed Peshmerga guerrillas could not defend Dohuk against the helicopter-gunships and multi-barrelled rocket-launchers of the Iraqi army.

The *Today* man withdrew to the village of Sansenk, about twenty kilometres north of Dohuk. He remembers sitting with a group of tired fighters, each cradling an AK47 assault rifle, when the rumour reached town that Dohuk had been recaptured and cleared of Iraqi forces. That was in the late evening. Carver and his friends went to bed that night intending to return to Dohuk at dawn.

By the time the sun rose a different story had reached Sansenk. This one was not an overoptimistic rumour. Saddam's tanks were coming up the valley. The entire population of the village was preparing to flee. Carver decided to go with them. He was terrified at the prospect of being caught by the Iraqis. 'It was a very low time and I don't mind admitting it. I was painfully aware that I had once been in the British Army. It hadn't taught me very much, except perhaps the basic field-craft, which allowed me to survive in the mountains, but I knew how the Iraqis would use it. I would be paraded as a hostage and accused of spying. The BBC could hardly deny that I had once been a soldier. It was true. And I knew the Iraqis would make no distinction between a former officer and a serving officer. I kept thinking of the way the civilian hostages had been used before the war. I knew how they would present me.'

For their onward transport he managed, with some Kurdish helpers, to obtain a dustcart. 'It was literally a domestic refuse truck. A bright orange van with less than 200 kilometres on the clock and a huge hopper on the back for collecting rubbish. We drove it northwards towards Zakho picking up refugees as we went – they just sat in the hopper behind the cab. We planned to head from Zakho up to the Turkish frontier. That was where the refugees were headed and I wanted to stick with them. It took all day to travel the hundred or so kilometres to Zakho. It was as if the whole world was on the road. There were old women with huge bundles on their backs, young boys on mules, old men sleeping beside the road using rocks for pillows. We gave lifts to everyone we could. At one point the back of the truck got so full that a father lost his baby. There was a huge commotion and we had to stop. Everyone got out. The baby was found, happily asleep, under several layers of blankets.'

But as they approached the outskirts of Zakho, the World Service news brought more alarming information. Iraqi troops had taken the town. As night fell, Carver could see the lights of their tanks and armoured vehicles patrolling the streets below him. 'We never quite reached Zakho. At a village just outside, a man pointed down the road and told us the Iraq tanks were just "down there". The only way out was to cross the mountains into Turkey. I looked up at the snow filled gullies and the jagged ridges above me. They looked pretty menacing.'

But that assumed they could get round Iraqi-occupied Zakho. Carver consulted his map. 'The problem was terrifying. There was no ring road. The route north from Zakho to the border appeared to branch off the road we were on right in the centre of town. At one point our driver, Cawa, refused to go any further. He was convinced we would get him killed. He only kept going because his fiancée was living in Zakho and he hoped to find her somewhere amongst the refugees fleeing the town.' Thoughts of capture, interrogation and perhaps even worse plagued Carver. He was convinced he was doomed. 'As the night wore on, our plight became increasingly desperate. The dustcart had no lights, so we drove by shining a torch out of the window and searched for the turning off to the mountains. Each pair of headlights that approached we thought was a tank.'

Luck was on his side. The road divided slightly earlier than his map suggested, on the outskirts of Zakho. There was no Iraqi patrol at the junction. Cawa turned the Mercedes dustcart onto the road leading up the valley from Zakho. With his adrenaline pumping furiously, Tom Carver found himself in a glacial valley a couple of miles wide. 'There were hundreds of little campfires. Each one marking the location of a family too exhausted to climb any further. Every so often Cawa stopped the dustcart to check if his girlfriend was among them.'

But many refugees had not stopped for the night. They were plodding relentlessly on towards the Turkish border. 'The road was packed with refugees. Eventually, a few miles short of the head of the valley, we came across a tidal wave of cars abandoned by fleeing Kurds. It was impossible to drive any further, so we just followed a trail of people trudging on foot. They had no food, no provisions, just the few possessions they could carry. I was utterly exhausted from a combination of terror and simple lack of sleep. By this time I had met a French press photographer. We agreed to try and get some rest. We slept where we fell, badly, and just for a few hours. I woke to a Biblical scene, thousands of Kurds just pushing on up towards the snow-line and the mountain ridge which was the Turkish border.' Carver particularly remembers the sight of an old woman in a wheelchair being pushed, relentlessly, through the snow. 'Her wheelchair was clanking, grinding and bumping. It must have taken a superhuman effort to keep moving her. But her family would not abandon her to the Iraqis. They just kept going, grinding through the snow. I can still hear the noise that wheelchair made. Just ten days earlier I'd reported from Kuwait about the misery of the Iraqi POWs, the sheer destruction on the highway to Basra. I had wondered whether the West hadn't been too harsh. Now I wondered why we let Saddam get away with so much.'

Eventually, after climbing for several miles, Carver and his companion reached the ridge. Thousands of Kurds were milling around confronted by young, frightened Turkish soldiers. The Turks were unmoved by the plight of the refugees. At least as hostile to Kurdish aspirations as the Iraqis, Turkey would not allow them to cross the border. The guards made it plain that they would fire if anyone attempted to pass them.

Carver and his French colleague were different. Their clothes and rucksacks stood out from the crowd. Unshaven and disreputable though they looked, they were clearly not poverty-stricken Kurds. A soldier summoned them forward. The Turks conferred briefly with their senior officers. Not much later a Turkish military helicopter landed on the ridge, and Carver was instructed to climb aboard. This was not a polite invitation. The Turks had no intention of leaving a BBC reporter on the ridge to witness their disregard for human rights. The helicopter ferried

Carver and the French photographer to a large military base at the foot of the mountains. Here Carver was briefly and lackadaisically interrogated. The Turks did not doubt that Tom Carver was who and what he said he was. They made it clear that he was free to go – as long as he did not try to get back to the refugees huddled on the ridge.

It was nearly midnight and Carver had only one thought: how was he going to file for the *Today* programme and for BBC news bulletins? There were telephones at the Turkish Army base but none of them seemed capable of making international calls. He faced a reporter's worst nightmare – an exclusive story of enormous importance and no obvious way to file it.

He begged and pleaded for help, and, while Turkish military bureaucracy plodded along, wrote a not entirely coherent version of what he had seen for BBC radio's midnight news bulletin. To his delight, a telephone capable of direct international dialling was located. It is not clear why the Turkish military, which had ordered a helicopter into action specifically to remove Carver from the scenes on the ridge, was now prepared to facilitate his efforts to report the experience. He did not bother to debate the point, just dialled News Traffic in London.

Carver filed his bulletin report first. Then Andrew Hawken, that night's duty editor on *Today*, came on the line to speak to his colleague and friend. Hawken's first concern was for Carver's personal well being. The reporter had been out of contact for days, missing in action. Since the arrival of the taped report smuggled out via Syria, nobody had heard a whisper from their man in Kurdistan. Concern had been growing that Carver might have been captured or killed.

To begin with, the reporter acknowledges, he was tense and incoherent. Hawken just took his time and listened to the whole story, from Damascus through to the helicopter ride. 'Right,' he said eventually. 'We'll just put you on live then.'

The 8.10 a.m. slot was allocated. No cabinet minister, no crafted package this time. For eighteen minutes, down a crackly but audible telephone line, Tom Carver just told his story to Brian Redhead.

He described seeing 'sights that I have never seen before and will never see again in my life', of 'children, barefoot, walking across snowfields ... old men trying to clamber up the rocky paths of the mountains ... old women just dressed in nighties.' The power of Tom Carver's report that morning was amplified by the raw emotion in his voice. He said he would never forget the look of 'sheer exhaustion and desperation on their faces', and explained that 'these people had no idea where they were going to end up ... they were being propelled by the sheer terror they felt for the army of Saddam Hussein.'

Wanting above all to spur political intervention that could assist the refugees, Carver told listeners that 'there are families at the top where the snow is covering everywhere, without a speck of protection, digging in the snow for enough water to make a cup of tea'. He described seeing one Kurdish woman giving birth to a child beside the mountain path, and told of children crying out in pain because they had no shoes and their feet were frozen, 'and, in the middle of it all, toddlers carrying their favourite lamb, an old man, hobbling along blind, another young mother, clearly about to give birth, hardly able to walk'.

Tom Carver had achieved what every good reporter hopes to achieve at least once in his career. He had been an eyewitness to history in the making. He brought the plight of the Iraqi Kurds to international attention. Andrew Hawken commented afterwards that 'Tom will have focused the attention of the government.' In the days that ensued, every newspaper in Britain followed up on his story.

'That interview,' says Carver simply, 'changed the whole agenda around the world. Within weeks we had the no-fly policy preventing Iraqi warplanes entering the northern and southern no-fly zones. That policy has been in place ever since. The Kurdish safe-havens were created. Operation Comfort was launched to bring relief to the refugees. The Kurds were badly let down later but I regard myself as lucky that I was able to bring the situation to world attention. It was worth it.'

The commitment the *Today* programme brought to enabling Carver to complete his mission is, it is worth observing, extremely rare. By conventional editorial criteria it was a hugely expensive way of filling a very small amount of airtime. With the exception of that lengthy eyewitness account to Brian Redhead, Tom Carver filed very little from northern Iraq. He was out of contact with base for days at a time. His colleagues at Broadcasting House were concerned about his safety, and many conversations took place in which the sole objective was to devise a way of telling Carver to come home. If communications had been better, Tom Carver would never have completed his mission. Only a few newspapers or commercial broadcasters would contemplate the investment this trip required without a reasonable certainty that their correspondent would file every day. Carver was under no pressure to do that – indeed, in no position to even try.

Carver himself was exhausted and drained by the time he reached Turkey. Conscious of the need to get more dramatic reporting for his money, his editor wanted him to stay in Turkey and to return to Kurdistan if possible. Tom Carver refused. He knew that every editor in Europe and America would be dispatching correspondents to cover the crisis on the Kurdish border. He had been there first. The pack could have the leftovers. He hired a taxi to take him to Ankara with the intention of flying straight home to London. It was an amusing end to a remarkable assignment. 'I had no clear idea where I was. I'd been single-minded about getting the story on the programme but I didn't really know where the helicopter had taken me. I thought Ankara was fairly close – you know, a few miles or so up the road. It was hundreds of miles away, a twelve-hour drive. When we got there, there were no flights to London for three days. I'd had enough, so I asked the driver to take me on to Istanbul [almost as far again as he had already travelled] so I could catch a flight there. He was overjoyed! His sister was getting married in Istanbul that weekend and I paid for his trip and probably most of the wedding too!'

My own first experience of taking big risks to obtain exclusive news for *Today* came a couple of years before the Gulf War. It was Christmas 1989. Like Carver, I went because Phil Harding asked me to – but if he had changed his mind, I would have pretended not to hear. My good fortune was that I did not travel alone. My first and most frightening foreign mission for *Today* was undertaken in the company of reporter Allan Little, now a veteran of the wars in Croatia, Bosnia and Rwanda, and one of the BBC's most respected correspondents.

Today sent us to Timisoara in Romania. Confused wire-reports had raised the possibility that Romania was about to overthrow its corrupt Communist dictator and follow Hungary, Czechoslovakia and East Germany down the path to liberation. Speculation about the fate of President Ceausescu had been aired on the programme that morning. *Today* was playing to its strengths, deploying the immediacy and power of radio to beat the lumbering juggernaut of television and the rigidity of news-paper deadlines. The editor, Phil Harding, was thinking laterally too. Bucharest was easier to reach than Timisoara – so BBC News would send dedicated correspondents there. But the city of Timisoara was almost certainly where the revolution had been made: more mysterious, more likely to reveal some of the truths behind the headlines, it was altogether a more *Today* programme destination.

Allan and I were not seasoned foreign correspondents. When we were asked to go, we could not even find Timisoara on the map. But we had both followed Phil Harding's instructions to carry passport, driving licence and credit cards at all times. He did not have to order us to surrender Christmas and abandon our families. He didn't need to. We were idealistic enough to regard the prospect of a revolution as a fantastic opportunity.

Seats on a flight from London to Belgrade were obtained within minutes by one of those unsung heroes of the *Today* pro-gramme – the programme assistants who make all the logistical arrangements that turn ideas into radio programmes but never get an on-air credit. There was hardly time to get to Heathrow. A colleague was ordered to collect £2000 in cash and take it to the airport where he threw it at me as we passed through the security check. Allan abandoned his VW Passat in a disabled parking space in the short-term car park at Terminal 2 (a fine amounting to several licence fees duly ensued). En route to Vienna we dis-cussed our rudimentary knowledge of Romania and then sweated while Yugoslav airlines threw two innocent citizens off the flight to Belgrade to make room for the men from the BBC.

Years later I remembered my confusion when the people of Vrsac insisted they were not Yugoslav but Serb. The wars of Yugoslav secession had not happened then and the little border town to which we had hastened from Belgrade airport seemed obsessed with an argument we did not understand. But Vrsac was just the staging post – a brief stop on the way to the border.

The barren ribbon of road separating the Yugoslav frontier post from its Romanian counterpart screamed cold war. Beyond the dilapidated huddle of Dacia cars pleading for admission to northern Serbia there was no traffic. Tank traps festooned the snow-speckled fields on either side. There was barbed wire coiled in the ditches. A crudely painted orange sign alerted drivers to the documentation required to enter Nicolae and Elena Ceausescu's ultra-Stalinist paradise. Tourist visas were required and had to be obtained from a Romanian Embassy or tourist Office, not at the border. Working visas for journalists were not mentioned. Forty-five years had passed since western reporters last turned up at the Romanian frontier unannounced.

Conventional bribes did not work instant magic. A grey-helmeted border guard took the proffered carton of Marlboro and ordered us to remain in the car. Then, a machine-gun cradled against his chest, he marched briskly back to join three colleagues, all similarly armed, who were gazing through binoculars at a group of men crouched in the field on the Romanian side of the border. These figures had guns too – AK47s – and briskly rejected what sounded like instructions to surrender them. Shouted negotiations continued. One of the Border Guards returned to his cabin to use a telephone – a gargantuan Bakelite thing which appeared to pre-date not just the transistor but the wireless set too.

The shouting intensified and the guards tensed. Marlboros were lit amid much checking of magazines. The man in the cabin emerged and consulted his colleagues. All four turned their backs on the men in the field and retreated into the cabin. They did not look back. Moments later, after a brief muttered conference in the freezing field, the fleeing Securitate men drifted away, heading on through the tank traps towards the Yugoslav frontier.

Four sets of blind eyes having been turned, attention could now focus on us. Every inch of our blue Audi hire car was subjected to intense scrutiny. The radio-cassette player and fuel-injected two-litre engine were objects of particular fascination. This was not a pure security check, more an extended pretext for young men to examine a product of western capitalism. So this was the sort of decadent junk that would infest their country if they ignored the orders of the self-styled 'genius of the Carpathians'. The atmosphere warmed considerably. Nobody needed to mention the obvious: that they had already committed treason by permitting the men with AK47's to walk across the border unmolested.

Much smoking took place in and around the car as a plethora of forms was extracted from the cabin. Names, passport numbers, professional credentials, car documents (which clearly decreed that the hire company would not permit the car to enter Romania, Albania, Bulgaria or the Soviet Union) were subjected to intimate scrutiny by men who spoke only a handful of English words. It was luminously clear that normal procedures had ceased to exist. Trusted communist soldiers, loyal enough to be posted to a venue within walking distance of Yugoslavia (then the most liberal, tolerant and prosperous of the totalitarian states) were making up new rules. They were imagining how border guards might behave at a frontier that was not formally sealed against the debilitating poison of freedom. Four young Romanians were re-inventing themselves before our eyes.

Nobody said we would be admitted. The power to say no was still a treasured asset to men who had nothing else. They must have considered impounding the car and sending us back to Vrsac on foot. But decency or premonitions about the future prevailed, and eventually the huge official stamps, without which no transaction in a communist state could be deemed complete, were produced. The stamps, seals and official endorsements granting consent to enter Timisoara Province in the Socialist Republic of Romania covered full pages in both our passports. Two cartons of Marlboro, £200 in cash and a bottle of Johnny Walker whisky had changed hands – and the difficult bit was still to come.

Once through the Romanian border the reality of revolution appeared at the roadside. Peasant boys with automatic rifles blocked the road and demanded identification. It became clear what was on their minds. The only people in Ceausescu's Romania who had access to fast cars were agents of the dreaded Securitate. Yugoslav number plates meant nothing. The Audi was stopped every mile or so by gun-toting adolescents in ragged clothes and plastic shoes. British passports seemed incomprehensible to them – though they seized them and stared – it was the little plastic BBC identity cards that did the trick. Time and again the passports were handed back amidst grinning faces, pointing fingers and spreading murmurs of 'BBC! BBC!' Only the Marlboro cigarettes bought in Belgrade were more popular. A single packet would mollify five teenagers. Professional soldiers wanted more.

As Little and I crawled towards Timisoara, Ceausescu and his wife were being air-lifted from the roof of the Central committee building in Bucharest by Major Vasile Malutan, 'the Danube of the thoughts' personal helicopter pilot. Beneath them, in Palace Square, crowds which had been dispersed by force the night before were chanting '*Ole, Ole, Ole, Ole Ceausescu nu mai e*' ('Ceausescu is no more').

Timisoara was infernal. Huge flames belched from an iron foundry, filling the air with acrid sulphurous fumes. A rusted metal arch in the shape of a shipbuilder's crane stood over the southern approach road. Looming above a crowd of ragged urchins whose presence proclaimed the reality of poverty, it declared the virtues of socialist labour. Beyond the children, men in civilian clothes ran as soldiers are trained to run, heads down, scurrying in short bursts between secure positions. They had guns.

Now there were no threats, just a high-energy cocktail of excitement and fear. This was the cradle of the Romanian Revolution, the town that had showed the capital what defiance meant. The rebels of Timisoara had made their choice. So had the soldiers ordered by Ceausescu to use live ammunition against them. Thirty-six hours earlier a crowd had marched into the town's Opera Square to demand that Ceausescu resign and the army side with the people. Among the conventional military commanders were some who knew what people power had done to recalcitrant communists in Berlin and Prague. Now the shooting, clearly audible from the centre of town, was between regular soldiers and die-hard agents of the Securitate. The revolution was not won – but the tide was turning. Everywhere the Romanian flag could be seen, with the red star of communism ripped from the centre.

No sink estate in Britain has ever looked like Timisoara. Crumbling apartment buildings thrown up with unfinished breeze blocks. Raw sewage in the mud-covered, cobbled streets. No private cars – just the tanks and armoured personnel carriers of the Romanian Army. Official shops which advertised generic basics – bread, milk and cheese – but had none. And then there was the fighting. Sober retrospective analysis has revealed that the Romanian revolution was as much a coup d'état as a popular uprising. But that was in Bucharest. In Timisoara people fought and died before the regime collapsed. We saw the evidence in the streets and the hospitals.

Radio Free Timisoara was our first base. We were directed there by a young drama student and follower of Claudiu Iordache, the banned playwright and author who had found himself at the head of the crowd in Opera Square on 20 December. Viorel's eyes shone with passion for change. He punched the air with enthusiasm as we witnessed a Securitate man captured and beaten by the mob in the street beneath a railway bridge. The hapless flunky knew he was doomed, as soon as he was recognized he clambered desperately up the metal struts of the bridge clawing frantically at the flaking metal to keep his feet above the grasping hands.

Radio Free Timisoara was an expression of hope. The premises of the former regional headquarters of Radio/Television Romania had been seized by young artists and idealists backed by uniformed soldiers of the Romanian army. Ceausescu clearly knew that Timisoara, with its vocal Hungarian minority, was not reliable, and the transmission studios had been stripped bare by the state when it centralized all broadcast programming in Bucharest. Now its new volunteers were hopeful that the honoured visitors from the BBC might somehow be able to make things work. We struggled to explain that we were journalists not technicians, capable of using technology but not building it.

Ammunition boxes were stacked on the floor and a nervous infantry officer maintained constant watches over the front and rear approaches to the building. He expected the Securitate would try to storm the place, and on the night of 23 December, while Allan Little lay on the floor with his tape recorder running, they tried but were repulsed by the disciplined fire-power within. During the quiet hours of that night the beautiful daughter of a Christian minister played her guitar and sang songs from the back catalogue of pre-war Romanian democracy – a perfect ingredient for the radio package we were constructing and a haunting counterpoint to the harsh crack of rifle fire. A few seconds of her voice were broadcast on *Today*. I still have a cassette of the whole song.

On Boxing Day 1989 the inhabitants of the radio building watched in awe as television pictures from Bucharest broadcast the hasty show trial and execution of Nicolae and Elena Ceausescu. The station director – still desperate to obtain the equipment with which to broadcast news to the region – watched in rapt silence before exploding in fury. He turned to me and through a mixture of beard and cigarette smoke bellowed in heavily accented English, 'It is wrong! Disgraceful!'

I nodded assent. 'Not the best way to begin building a democracy.'

'No, no! Not that!' he screamed in contempt. 'They should have tortured them! Shooting was too good. Too kind! They should have made them suffer like those bastards made us suffer.' Nobody disagreed.

At Timisoara's Hospital Clinic Number One we found Dr Aurel Mogoseanu on the edge of despair. He had nearly thirty victims of gunshot wounds in his trauma ward, but no disposable syringes, tiny quantities of crude anaesthetic and one ancient respirator held together with insulating tape. The respirator was allocated to an Italian journalist. He had been shot in the chest and had not regained consciousness.

With impressive dignity Dr Mogoseanu, a surgeon who had trained in Chicago and knew what modern medicine could do, described how he had organized treatment of the wounded during the first days of the revolution. There were few other surgeons willing to assist him. The regime had not yet fallen and Party members were unwilling to risk their futures by repairing damage the dictator had ordered. He had operated in an open ward with obstetricians, general practitioners, midwives and casualty nurses lined up beside him. He had conducted the most complex surgery while instructing his apprentices on each step of their procedures. There had been terrible problems with sterile equipment, local anaesthetics had been applied where general ones were patently needed, but most of the patients had made it. The Italian reporter had been Mogoseanu's own patient. His wounds were clean and bandaged. The surgeon did not expect him to live.

'We needed a proper respirator but we did not have one that worked.' He shrugged. 'I did my very best.' It was as if he expected us to be angry about his efforts for one of our media colleagues. Mollified that we were not, he took us into a side ward and pointed at a row of gun-metal grey machines. The silver identification plaques revealed they were British made. But none had the sealed glass cylinder they required to work. Could we order some from the manufacturer? Reluctant to express our concern that these were examples of 1950's technology – dubious even that the manufacturers would still exist – we noted make and model.

At Timisoara's showpiece Intercontinental Hotel, Allan and I were allocated rooms on the thirteenth floor. The soldiers at reception were adamant about this – although they were not at all sure the lifts would work. It meant our accommodation was above the roofs of the surrounding buildings. If the Securitate attacked the hotel, and they had done so repeatedly, their shots would be travelling upwards. As long as we stayed away from the windows, we would be safe from anything except stray ricochets.

Today does not expect to break news of the type Tom Carver broke from Kurdistan. Rather it is an oasis of exploration and debate. Comparing the programme to a broadsheet newspaper misses the point – that *Today* is not comprehensive. It does not attempt the breadth of coverage provided by newspaper editors. In fact, it has more in common with publications like *The Economist*, *Time* or *Newsweek*. Its success depends upon the ruthless selection of a tiny number of elements from a plethora of possibilities. It is this weeding, the editorial instinct to disregard all but the most intriguing, controversial or plain eccentric items, which makes the programme special, and which gave the reports Allan Little and I compiled in Timisoara their impact. We were not burdened with the conventional journalists' need for instant facts and figures. We had time in which to assess and contextualize what we saw before we filed.

Thousands had been killed in Timisoara – that was what the army and the hospital told us. We visited the scenes of alleged violence, talked to soldiers when we were not sure which side they were on, assessed the revolutionary propaganda, and asked ourselves whether such casualty claims were really plausible.

The truth of the matter, we were eventually to report, was that they were not. Revolutionaries had offered up an eviscerated corpse as evidence that the Securitate had bayoneted pregnant women – the story appeared in sensationalist newspapers across Europe. In miserable fact, we discovered, it was that of a woman who had died during a failed caesarean section. Her body had been extracted from the hospital morgue for the delectation of journalists. Rumour built upon fantasy had created a wildly inflated death toll. In a city the size of Timisoara, 2000 deaths would have meant that every citizen of the town would know someone who had been killed.

The reports Allan Little and I filed from Timisoara helped *Today* to win the acclaimed Sony Award for 'Best coverage of a News Event' for its treatment of the revolution in Romania. Despite our inexperience, the programme's ethos had helped us to look for the first glimmerings of truth about what was really going on in Ceausescu's vile experiment with ultra-orthodox Stalinism. Like Tom Carver later, and with considerably less justification, we were both scared by the experience. But we knew that what we were doing would have a much greater impact than the work of individual newspaper reporters who reached Timisoara forty-eight hours behind us.

Today gets more than diligence from its journalists. It inspires excellence because it sets such high standards. Tom Carver might not have risked his life to highlight the plight of Iraqi Kurds if he had not been certain that his work would make an impact. Mike Williams, the *Today* programme's full-time foreign correspondent who remained in Belgrade throughout the NATO campaign to expel Slobodan Milosevic from Kosovo, felt the same way.

There are two other factors in this process. The first is money. Editors at rival publications and programmes point out that *Today* is hugely well financed, that it has the luxury of public money with which to fund expeditions others cannot justify. Having since tried to provide comprehensive foreign news coverage as a newspaper editor in a relentlessly competitive market, I understand just how fortunate BBC editors are in this respect. They have the incomparable good fortune to be able to experiment and make mistakes. *Today* is able to spend its way to excellence with a generosity few can match. Many critics argue that this creates a distortion in the market for news, and they are right to argue that it should experiment more often if its privileges are to be maintained.

The other crucial factor is the audience. *Today* listeners are so dedicated, so well informed, so loyal to the programme that extra effort is always rewarded by letters and calls of appreciation. They may not wholly justify being shelled by the Iraqi army – but sometimes they come quite close.

No other current affairs programme in radio or television has managed to create the same sense of team pride among its staff. A few quality newspapers have achieved it – the *Guardian*, *Daily Mail*, *The Economist* and *Washington Post* perhaps – but there is one final difference, one factor that ensures *Today* still stands out from the pack. It is that every *Today* staffer knows their work will be heard by all their competitors. *Guardian* journalists may not always read the *Mail*, but *Today* reports are heard by all of them. If the attention of your peers is a powerful motivator, then *Today* staff are the most highly motivated in British journalism.

It is no coincidence, however, that the *Today* programme these days contains significantly less original foreign news reporting than ten years ago. Shortly after I returned to London from the Gulf War, the BBC gave me a little plastic card. Apparently designed to introduce me to the concept of health and safety concerns, it asked, among other things, whether there was a danger of war or civil disorder in the region I was planning to visit. I remember thinking, 'There would have been absolutely no point going if the answer had been no.' I assume Tom Carver felt the same way. There is no future in *Today* if it does not have the courage to sponsor risk-taking. That reality causes constant headaches to the army of BBC bureaucrats who think about insurance claims and risk assessments before they think about stories.

SEVEN

'Thought for the Day'

There is one fixed point, one *Today* institution, which attracts considerable affection from listeners while remaining almost incomprehensible to staff. It is 'Thought for the Day', those three minutes of unchallenged theological and philosophical reflection which appear at 7.50 each morning. Although they have too much sensitivity (and fear of BBC management) to say so in public, most programme staff detest it. At best they refer to it as simply 'Thought'; more often disparagingly as 'the God slot'. For one *Today* presenter it is merely 'some priest wittering on'.

Editors and producers rarely pay the remotest attention to what is said by contributors to 'Thought for the Day'. Asked what it is for, one *Today* producer looked pensive: 'It's a great chance to grab a cup of coffee. We couldn't care less what's in it. It's a total waste of three minutes of prime airtime. I'm sure thousands of listeners just switch off, go into the shower, brush their teeth or do something else while whoever it is burbles on. It's antediluvian. Crass. It has no place in a serious news and current affairs programme. Can you imagine anyone putting a God slot in *Newsnight* or *Channel Four News*? You might as well suggest using a topless newsreader.'

Successive editors of the *Today* programme have deliberately failed to act on this perception. Jenny Abramsky commissioned research which showed that many listeners considered it too long and rambling and switched off or changed channels while it was on. But that same research also indicated that 'the God slot' was more popular than *Today*'s sport and business slots. So she cut 'Thought for the Day' from four and a half minutes' duration to just three minutes.

For most of the *Today* team, though, the survival of

'Thought' has nothing to do with popularity. They would agree with the *Guardian*'s Polly Toynbee that its survival is 'purely BBC politics. The BBC has an obligation to do a certain amount of religion. Removing it would cause a huge stink.' In other words, the BBC keeps 'Thought for the Day' because without it the Corporation might face renewed pressure to dedicate other chunks of valuable airtime to religion – and that would be a ratings disaster. 'Thought for the Day', in this analysis, has become a repository for the BBC's last gesture towards the delusion that Britain is still a religious country, a lingering relic of the BBC's role as a cornerstone of the post-war British establishment. Many hoped that John Birt would abolish it – as Deputy Director General he was known to have doubts about it – but as Director General he had a change of mind. 'I think it works extremely well,' he eventually declared. 'It's a sort of pause for reflection, a different quality of thought … I find it engaging and enjoyable.'

The producer who regarded it as a good opportunity for a coffee break raises his eyebrows ceiling-wards. 'A different quality of thought? How about the total absence of thought? We are journalists. We are not supposed to believe anything for which there is no objective evidence. And we plop a propaganda broadcast for people who insist there is a god right in the middle of *Today*? Bizarre.'

Humanists share that perception. The British humanist movement waged a four-decade long campaign to include the views of atheists in 'Thought for the Day'. In recent years that thinking has moved on. Like the majority of *Today* staff, some humanists now argue that the right approach would be to scrap the item altogether – that it allows representatives of minority viewpoints unchallenged access to a powerful medium, and is not subjected to any of the rigorous editorial tests applied to the rest of *Today*'s content.

And yet. The contempt with which 'Thought' is regarded by *Today* staff is mirrored by the reverence attached to it in religious circles and the attention paid to it in the press. Perhaps, if something as anachronistic as 'Thought for the Day' did not exist, the *Today* programme would have to invent it. As the programme has become more confident of its status as Britain's premier outlet for incisive broadcast journalism, so it has lost some of the humour, character and lightness of touch many listeners clearly adore. David Coomes, executive producer of 'Thought for the Day', is certain that *Today*'s agenda has become harder, more determinedly political since Redhead died, 'and in that context "Thought" matters even more than it used to'. It has allowed the programme to preserve elements of the type of eccentricity that was once provided by presenters like Jack de Manio, John Timpson, Brian Redhead and Peter Hobday.

Secondly, argues Christina Odone, deputy editor of the *New Statesman* and, as one of Britain's leading lay Catholics, a regular contributor to 'Thought for the Day', 'In a secular and multi-cultural society, which is how I would describe Britain, it is quite important and actually very interesting to hear people who still cling to the so-called traditional faiths, to have their take on what is going on. Nobody ever mentions the age-old beliefs. Nobody ever mentions morality. Nobody ever mentions our need to be judged and to judge because, in this very relativist society, people are scared of being condemned as bigoted the moment they talk about God or being condemned as prejudiced the moment they talk about "my faith".'

'Religion and the *Today* programme do not go hand in hand,' she goes on to assert. 'It is not tremendously interested in the spiritual life unless it is touchy-feely New Ageism. It is so very much part of a self-conscious anti-establishment, which is, in truth, really the new establishment, a north London, liberal-thinking, left-wingish kind of community.'

Odone therefore relishes the extent to which, in her opinion, 'Thought' challenges the very principles on which *Today* journalists produce the show. 'Radio Four is about reaching the chattering classes and middle England, but the *Today* programme is very much about the chattering classes and the media. *Today* is a constant in the media world – I have never sat at an editorial meeting where the *Today* programme is not brought up. So, because it is not middle England but the media that the *Today* programme plays to, it follows as night follows day, that there is an anti-Christian, anti-religious element to it.'

Britain's Chief Rabbi, Dr Jonathan Sacks, also a regular contributor, agrees. 'Cultural elites in the west are more anti-religious than the total population. In Britain, the USA, most of Europe and in the state of Israel the media are immensely anti-religious, secularist, not just secular. There are religious people in the media, the late Brian Redhead with whom I first did the *Today* programme was a deeply religious individual and spoke and wrote about it. But, taken as a whole, it's a very beautiful thing that "Thought for the Day" lets one enter in this dissident voice which says, "Hang on – not everything that is real is captured by the daily news."'

Polly Toynbee rejects this view with amused contempt. 'If you want to do it,' she argues, 'you should do it as religion hard-headed. I would like them to do preaching. I wouldn't mind readings out of the Koran, the bible. What I can't bear is this need to make it relevant. This picking up, in a mushy way, of hard-headed news events and saying, "From this we can learn."' For her that is 'soft-headed, soft-brained re-warming with a bit of opinion and a great deal of banality, which, up against the hard pressure of events, news, politics, real life, just sounds very odd and pretty pathetic. The tone of voice changes and you think, "Oh God, it's that", and you immediately switch off.

'On the whole it's pretty much consensus ridden. You occasionally have Jonathan Sacks or someone, but it leans towards decent Methodists, nice people. It doesn't really give you a feel for what much religion is like. You don't get a sense for the cut and thrust and blood of where these faiths all meet each other in antagonism in other parts of the world, in India or Ireland or the Middle East, where religion matters. What you get is the detritus of religion in a country where it no longer matters at all.'

Popular or merely convenient, like the rest of *Today* 'Thought' has the power to attract big names. On 1 January 2000 the new millennium was marked by what the BBC proudly described as 'a person of sufficient standing to fill this prestigious slot'. Allocated a little more than the customary three minutes, Prince Charles greeted a generally hungover United Kingdom with his views on the significance of the millennium, the power of its symbolism and the 'sacred basis of our existence'. The broadcast was deemed a success. It certainly helped the Prince to emphasize his serious approach to what, for many, was a time for unthinking revelry. He had declined to attend the government-sponsored festivities at the now notorious Dome, spending New Year's Eve touring hostels for the homeless in Scotland instead. His 'Thought for the Day' was recorded in advance, just as his mother's Christmas Broadcast always is.

So 'Thought' can be high status. Occasionally it is simply provocative, encouraging the sort of views that, as Christina Odone observes, rarely appear in the rest of the *Today* programme. The most controversial example of this power to shock by ignoring the rules of political correctness occurred on 10 October 1996 when Anne Atkins, still at that time a relatively inconspicuous Vicar's wife from West London, delivered a ferocious denunciation of the Church of England's attitude towards homosexuality.

The liberal establishment was, predictably, incensed. Atkins was accused of homophobia, of 'slagging off' gays and 'calling down the wrath of God on homosexuals'. She was also contracted to write an agony column for the *Daily Telegraph* and generally congratulated by other bastions of 'traditional values'.

In fact, as is so often the case with live radio, the screams of outrage were aimed at what listeners *imagined* Atkins to have said, not at what she actually *did* say. It is extraordinary how often this happens. Listeners do not take shorthand notes, nor do they record items. They react to an impression conveyed by a tone of voice or the general tenor of an argument and regularly make the mistake of objecting to words which were simply not uttered, or at least not in the order or context they believe they heard them.

Anne Atkins was a classic victim. Her real message was that the Church of England could not be surprised if the number of candidates for ordination was falling – as it certainly was – if it refused to adhere to Christian teaching. She accurately summarized this teaching as being that 'God loves the sinner but hates the sin.' From this she argued that the Church should love and care for homosexuals, should welcome them into its congregations, but should not hesitate to condemn homosexual practices.

Having deliberately stirred indignation with the provocative suggestion that the Church might as well 'have an Adulterer's Christian Fellowship or a Sex Before Marriage Christian Fellowship' as celebrate the twentieth anniversary of the Lesbian and Gay Christian Movement, Atkins concluded with the thought that 'If the trumpet sounds an uncertain note, who will prepare for battle? Sadly the note from the Church of England today is so uncertain, you'd think it was from a cracked penny whistle.'

Nobody paid much attention to her trenchant declaration that 'Homophobia is reprehensible', nor her clear statement that 'discriminating against people on the grounds of their sexual orientation, which they may not have chosen, is indefensible'. Atkins had put her head above the parapet to express a view that was widely shared by traditional Christians. She had dared to articulate thoughts that may not be spoken in 'progressive' company.

The *Daily Telegraph, Spectator* and *Daily Mail* were overjoyed. As far as they were concerned, Atkins had scripture on her side. Other Christians might want to accept homosexual activity. Some parishes might actively do so. Their view was that Atkins had hit the bull's eye. Christian teaching did condemn homosexuality, whether gays and their supporters liked it or not.

The Church of England fanned the flames. Conducting itself as if it had never heard of the notion that democrats are supposed to be able to 'hate what you say' while 'defending to the death your right to say it', it came perilously close to suggesting that the BBC should have censored Anne Atkins for daring to think such things. The Reverend Eric Shegog, the Church's Director of Communications, wrote a furious epistle to the editor of *Today* and the head of BBC Religious Broadcasting. He declared that it was 'preposterous' of Atkins to claim that the decline in new ordinands was a result of the Church of England's tolerance of homosexuality (he overlooked the fact that many clergymen contacted the BBC to say that it was a very likely cause). The church demanded an apology and protested that it had not been offered 'an immediate right of reply'.

It was Christina Odone's argument in action: liberals denouncing 'Thought for the Day' because they did not like the contents. But this time the liberals were in the traditionally 'Thought' supporting classes. It does not appear to have crossed any of their minds that, had Anne Atkins' script had been diluted or had an opponent been invited to interrogate her about it before she had finished speaking, the whole basis of 'Thought for the Day' would have crumbled. Anne Atkins's legendary contribution was 'Thought' at its best. It provoked controversy and did what the rest of *Today*'s journalism always seeks to do by setting a story running in the newspapers.

The problem with 'Thought', however, is too rarely the controversy it provokes and more often the frequency with which it promotes somnolence in the listener. January 2000 was not the first time the Prince of Wales blessed the nation with the fruit of his innermost musings from the pulpit of the *Today* programme. A precedent had been set on 8 May 1995 when he broadcast to commemorate the 50th anniversary of VE Day. This was an example of 'Thought for the Day' at its facile, meandering worst. Charles seemed more concerned to avoid giving offence than to actually say anything interesting. He reflected on the 'bravery, chivalry and romance' conveyed to him by his parents' stories about the war, shared his view that in this 'earthly existence … everything consists of opposites. There is good and there is evil. There is death and there is also life', and observed that some 'civilized values in our country are a reflection of our Christian inheritance'. He also took great care to remember that people 'of many different religions' gave their lives during the war.

Moral philosophy it was not, though it was certainly well intended. Prince Charles had an excuse. He could not afford to cause offence while encouraging the nation to remember those who had given their lives in the cause of freedom. While he may be prepared to arouse controversy on the subject of genetically modified food or modern architecture, the future head of the established church can ill-afford to make enemies in the spiritual arena. But his performance illustrated 'Thought for the Day's' problem perfectly. David Coomes, the slot's current editor, himself admits that 'there are moments when "Thought for the Day" comes on and I have to turn it off myself. It can be extremely embarrassing sometimes, in the middle of a hard news programme, when certain scripts come on. On Saturdays I think you can get away with a softer script. Monday to Friday you certainly can't. I think we put ourselves in danger sometimes with one or two scripts which, if Greg Dyke heard it, puts us in the shit, frankly.'

One antidote has been the much-resented culling of 'Thought' contributors. In April 1996 the Venerable George Austin, Father Oliver McTernan, Dr Donald English, John Newbury, Canon Philip Crowe, the Bishop of Oxford and Dr Leslie Griffiths were simultaneously informed that they would not be required again in the immediate future. They were not dismissed for ever. But the immediate message was unambiguous – don't call us, we'll call you.

The subsequent fuss is proof positive of the importance attached to 'Thought for the Day' by the British Christian churches. Much was made of the fact that all seven of the victims were Christian clergymen. Theologians and friends of the 'Thought for the Day Seven' were mobilized to protest. The BBC was accused of rejecting the Christian viewpoint, pretending that all religions are the same, treating senior religious leaders as if they were third rate actors, and, quite ludicrously, of clearing out controversial broadcasters in advance of a general election. A few of the victims had the humility to consider that they might have been dropped because they were no longer interesting. The majority appear to have lacked that basic Christian virtue.

David Coomes was the target of real hostility. 'We had lots and lots of correspondence at that time – letters from the denominations concerned and a lot from listeners, particularly if their favourite contributor was one of those rested. It became a huge problem, not only for the participants who were rested but for their communities as well.' He does not deny that he handled the affair clumsily, but maintains that 'some people had become a little complacent or just tedious and we had to bring in some new blood'.

That is precisely what happened. The modern 'Thought' is not as dominated by Christian denominations as it once was. Now contributors are selected from a pool of thirty approved names, which include representatives of most branches of the Christian faith, one Muslim, a popular Sikh (Indarjit Singh), one Hindu, two orthodox Jews and a reform Jew. Coomes regrets that he has not been able to find a Buddhist. 'It's quite difficult to get the Buddhist perspective to give a hard nosed "Thought" because the way they think about things tends to be rather soft and gentle.'

Nor does the team at BBC religion assume that individual contributors can remain interesting if they are used too often. Coomes says 'Once upon a time we had regulars doing Monday and Friday and one person did Tuesday, Wednesday and Thursday. We dropped that when it became obvious that someone did quite well on Tuesday and perhaps on Wednesday but by Thursday they didn't have much to say. So, we gave people four Tuesdays or four Thursdays with a whole week in between, and that did help.'

Despite the changes, now sufficiently bedded in to allow some of those culled in 1996 to make return appearances on 'Thought for the Day', David Coomes confesses that he is not entirely happy with his line up. 'We are constantly looking for new people. People who can do "Prayer for the Day" or "Pause for Thought" or preach good sermons or rap from a soapbox somewhere are not necessarily those who can do "Thought for the Day". It's quite difficult.'

The BBC's Religious Affairs Department has a concise definition of what 'Thought for the Day' should be about. The slot is an opportunity to 'reflect from a perspective of religious faith on the sort of issues, topics and people with which the *Today* programme deals'. Contributions are submitted in advance in an attempt to make sure they meet the required standard. Occasionally they are censored. Christina Odone admits she has been persuaded to drop things from her proposed broadcasts – 'I have been known to be too vicious about the Archbishop of Canterbury.'

Being excessively forthright may occasionally cause ripples. The more common fault in 'Thought' is sitting so firmly on the fence that it says nothing at all. A perfect example is a 'Thought for the Day' broadcast by the Anglican Bishop of Oxford on 5 November 1999. *The Times* had previously alleged that he was calling on the Church of England to address God as Mother. He had, of course, done nothing of the sort, but when he used the 'Thought' slot to deny the allegation, his principal concern appears to have been to avoid offending any listeners who might think it appropriate to call God she. 'The Divine Mystery,' he contended, 'is no more masculine than feminine and the godhead includes all the best characteristics of fatherhood and mother-hood. But because the scriptures not only in Christianity but in Judaism and Islam concentrate on addressing God as Father, it would understandably be very unsettling to address God as Mother in public worship.' The possibility was left wide open that it might be entirely appropriate to use such terms in private worship. The Bishop did not pursue that line of argument. 'Nevertheless [a word normally a precursor to vacillation], I think that for this very reason it is all the more important to make use of metaphors and images in the scriptures that draw out the feminine side of divine love.' In conclusion he advised his listeners to consider God as a father who 'includes within himself all the qualities that we associate with maternal love', because 'He is a father who loves like a mother.'

This type of pinhead samba may make sense to the minority of *Today*'s audience who participate in debate about divine gender. It is difficult to see how it relates to the requirement to pass spiritual or religious comment on a topical issue. For whom was the gender of God a topical debating point? For most Britons getting out of bed and preparing for the day ahead, it seems unlikely to have provoked a moment's contemplation.

Failing to be relevant is a common problem. But compare the utterly bizarre anecdotes recounted by some 'Thought' contributors. On 10 March 2001 Canon Eric James broadcast a 'Thought' so eccentric, so obviously not about a topical issue, that one wonders how it survived the censors. His argument was convoluted but, in essence, sought to suggest that a Bishop who swore loudly when a workman dropped a heavy pipe on his foot during a confirmation service demonstrated the somewhat obscure assertion that humour is one of the reasons we should believe in God.

'Mark Twain said categorically,' concluded Canon James, '– as if he had particular reason to know – "There is no humour in heaven." I beg to differ. I believe that the God who created us with a sense of humour will have prepared for us in heaven new and unexpected ways of revealing it. Heaven without humour wouldn't be heaven.'

This type of homily would never pass the scrutiny of a newspaper editor. Rod Liddle, the present editor of *Today*, says it would never pass his scrutiny either. 'It is too often just mean-dering and anecdotal. A few contributors can do anecdotes well, Lionel Blue sometimes does. Most can't.'

Rabbi Lionel Blue. It is impossible to write about 'Thought for the Day' without considering the contributions made by this gay Rabbi from the East End of London. Lionel Blue was born in 1930. His early memories involve the vicious street fighting which occurred near his home between the black-shirted British Union of Fascists and their Communist opponents. He left the ghetto to read history at Oxford and was ordained as a Rabbi in 1960.

Nothing in Blue's formal religious career has had anything approaching the impact of his appearances on the *Today* pro-gramme. The Catholic contributor Angela Tilby once said of Blue that he was, 'a writer, a teacher, a friend, a maverick, an "ecumaniac" but, above all, a broadcaster'. Until Blue delivered the first of several hundred 'Thoughts of the Day', he was completely anonymous, and the Jewish religious presence on British radio had been confined to the annual occasion on which the Chief Rabbi gave his Passover speech – deliberately directed at conventionally observant members of the Jewish community.

Lionel Blue speaks to a broader world. He admits that he has great difficulty believing in an external god at all, and explains that 'in a Jewish family, even if you do not believe a thing, even if you say you are an atheist, it never occurs to you not to light the Sabbath candles or not to keep kosher food laws. This is both the strength of Judaism and its difficulty ... I am not good at belief.' This candour about his problems with faith has made Blue a very sympathetic figure to millions of listeners.

He does not try to make religion simple. Nor does he attempt to reduce morality to absolute commands. Blue speaks cheerfully about his own confusion. He compares his quest for God with looking for fairies under the bed, and says that his early training in critical, analytical thought caused him to conclude that neither God nor the fairies existed. He had a youthful flirtation with Communism and was powerfully influenced by Stalinist and Trotskyite members of his family. After that came university, religious confusion and a tortuous coming to terms with his own sexuality.

Blue knows how eagerly anticipated his 'Thought for the Day' slots are and confesses that he agonizes over each contribution. 'I have to put an awful lot of thought into it. If you are giving a sermon for half an hour, somewhere along the line you and your message are going to bump into each other. But if you have only got two and a half minutes flat, you jolly well have to know what you are trying to say and you have to be careful about it.'

Lionel Blue manages to hit the mark on almost every occasion. But he is not a natural communicator who simply blossoms in front of a microphone. His chirpy, sugar sweet, 'Hello Sue, Hello John, Hello everybody' (parodied by crueller members of the *Today* staff as 'Hello, sky, hello, flowers, I'm Rabbi Fotherington-Thomas and there are fairies at the bottom of my garden') may convey an air of relaxed calm, but the humour, elegance and sheer friendliness of his contributions masks the obvious effort behind them.

I remember sweating and panicking for him on the morning when he found himself without a script. He had photocopied his 'Thought' in the *Today* office before coming into the studio. Page one flowed smoothly as ever, but when he reached for page two, Blue realized he had brought two copies of the first page and none of the second. For several agonizing seconds – which during a live broadcast always seem to last for eternity – he was flummoxed, opening and shutting his mouth like a beached cod and flapping his hands in panic. Only when prompted by a presenter did he attempt to summarize what he had written from memory. He ad-libbed for about thirty seconds before drying up.

It was an important insight. Lionel Blue has struggled to be as good as he is as a broadcaster. The warmth and humanity are all utterly real but the performance must exhaust him. He admits that he is a rather neurotic personality, that 'any bit of faith I have ever acquired has been acquired the hard way', and that not every member of the Jewish community appreciates his ability to reach out to Christians, Buddhists, Muslims and atheists too.

Blue is clear about his approach and well aware that some

people find it controversial. He has explained that 'some Jews complain and say, "Rabbi Blue goes too much with Christians." But the truth is, if Christians like you, and you are on the Christian radio and Christians listen, then you become respectable among Jews too… they always have one eye on the Christian world and are trying to see what it thinks.' Blue takes the controversial view that 'as far as European Judaism is concerned, our existence depends upon whether we can find a purpose in the largely Christian or post-Christian pluralist society in which we live.'

This conscious ecumenicism and overt liberalism are what make Lionel Blue the perfect contributor to 'Thought for the Day'. A Rabbi who admits he has had 'several long-term religious affairs' with other faiths (including Marxism, anarchism, Vedanta, analysis and therapy), he is perfectly placed to respond to the *Today* audience's ambivalence about conventional religion. Blue is spiritual without being remotely orthodox. He talks about human dilemmas, rarely about theology and regards Christianity as over-intellectualized, a faith searching for certainty in a world dominated by ambiguity and confusion.

If Ann Atkins's theological rigour can offend and infuriate the *Today* audience, Lionel Blue's cuddly eccentricity envelops them in a warm duvet of tolerance. His very existence is proof that, for at least some obviously intelligent folk, hard questions do not require hard answers. Atkins might reasonably contend that being a Rabbi and a practising homosexual are theologically incompatible. Blue's response to such rigidity is that 'Jewish Rabbis are not quite like priests… . A Rabbi has to be efficient, and he has to be hard-working and he has to be bright. Whether he has to be saintly is debatable. But certainly one thing he must not do is to bore his congregation. What I have done [by coming out as gay] has not bored them. It has been the talk of Golders Green for years and has kept everybody in chit-chat for a long time!'

Rabbi Blue appals religious fundamentalists. He is controversial among more orthodox sections of the Jewish community. But he has become almost as adored as the presenters to many *Today* listeners. Polls and anecdotes combine to prove that Lionel Blue is the most widely recognized member of the

'Thought' team. His name and his views are listened to by many *Today* regulars who ignore every other contribution to 'Thought for the Day'. He represents a perfect blend of the spirituality Christina Odone adores and the secular liberalism of Polly Toynbee.

In the opinion of Britain's Chief Rabbi, Dr Jonathan Sacks, '"Thought for the Day" has performed a unique service, which I don't think anyone has fully realized.' It has done nothing less than help 'preserve Britain's character as a tolerant society, [and] to move that tolerance from a predominantly Christian, Church of England society as Britain was between 1850 and 1950 to the more multi-cultural society it is.

'Take the Jewish community,' continues Dr Sacks, 'a very small community, very concerned with its own issues, with security, possible physical attack, with anti-Semitism, Jewish marriage and inter-marriage. Now, what allows a community like that to look outward as a community? Well, when I do "Thought for the Day" I'm talking as a Jew to an audience which is 99.5 per cent non-Jewish. I therefore have to develop a language that I would never, ever have to use otherwise. It's an inclusive language. It's a language which has to be accessible to people who don't share my terms of reference. And that has done (a lot) for me as surely it has done for Indarjit Singh and the Sikh community and other religious communities. It makes each of those communities feel we are a voice in the national conversation.'

During an interview for this book, I asked Dr Sacks to justify the inclusion of an unmediated religious perspective in Britain's leading news and current affairs programme. He did so with genuine intellectual rigour. But the simple act of asking clearly forced the Chief Rabbi to think about the possibility of *Today* without 'Thought'. In his next 'Thought for the Day', on Monday, 26 March 2001, he broadcast a trenchant and affectionate defence of the slot. When I asked David Coomes why Dr Sacks had chosen the slot itself as his subject – and why such an apparently non news-related topic had been accepted by the production team – he explained that Dr Sacks had been perturbed that anyone might consider 'Thought' superfluous to requirements. He wanted to send a message the Director General would hear. This is what Jonathan Sacks said:

The other day I was phoned up by a gentleman who wanted to know what I thought about the Today Programme. He's writing the official history [*sic*] and he wanted to know my views. Well, what could I say except that I can't think of a better way of being woken up on a Monday morning than by the gracious tones of Sue MacGregor or the good-natured bolshiness of a John Humphrys or a James Naughtie. I'm a fan, and have been since the days of Jack de Manio, who always got the time wrong, and the late Brian Redhead, one of the greatest masters radio ever had. And then he wanted to know what I thought about 'Thought for the Day'.

'Isn't it a bid odd,' he said, 'to have a kind of mini-sermon in the middle of a news programme?'

'Totally,' I said, 'it's wacky, eccentric and wholly benign, exactly like everything else that's great in British culture.' There's nothing odder than the British constitution, and yet for centuries it's been the world's living tutorial in how to create a free society. There's nothing odder than the shape of a London taxi or the giant ferris wheel called the London Eye, but we love them both and we wouldn't have them any other way. Odd is what gives character to a country.

And then I got serious, because 'Thought for the Day' does two things that are very serious indeed. Firstly, it's made an enormous contribution to our multi-faith society. When I speak in a synagogue, I'm talking to people like me. But right now I'm talking to an audience, most of whom aren't Jewish: and that means I have to speak in a way that spans differences and communicates across boundaries. That's a habit we all have to learn if we're going to be true to ourselves and yet make space for the people who aren't like us. That's what 'Thought for the Day' forces people like me to do, and Britain is the better because of it.

Secondly, it reminds us that there is something beyond the news. It's called perspective. The news is about today. But the great faiths remind us of yesterday and tomorrow. They're our living dialogue with the past and the future; those two essential things called memory and hope. There's nothing more guaranteed to make us make the wrong decisions than to live solely in the present, forgetting the lessons of the past and our duty to generations not yet born. So, in a world of sound bites and ever-decreasing attention spans, it doesn't hurt to have a daily reminder of eternity. That, at any rate, is my thought for the day.'

In truth, the BBC is not likely to drop 'Thought'. David Coomes believes there is an even stronger reason than its charm, eccentricity and change of perspective. 'At its very best, "Thought" captures the mood of the nation at times of crisis or disaster.'

This is what it did on the Monday after the Real IRA bombing of Omagh, when the production team found a local priest who had been counselling the victims and their families and persuaded him to write 'Thought for the Day'. He did it brilliantly, as did Richard Harries, the Bishop of Oxford, who contributed a 'Thought' to the special Sunday edition of *Today* that marked the death of Princess Diana. (David Coomes had wanted the Archbishop of Canterbury, but George Carey was apparently reluctant – a surprising attitude for the spiritual head of the Church of England.)

But these are special occasions, times when a reflective or spiritual perspective is clearly desirable. Besides the feeling, common in BBC News and Current Affairs, that 'Thought for the Day' does not deserve the profile it gets at 7.50 a.m. and should move to a less critical time, it is also facing a second threat – though some might see it as an opportunity. This view, slowly gaining currency among certain sections of BBC management, is that it need not always be religious. Rod Liddle has pioneered an experiment in what 'Thought for the Day' could become if it never tolerated the nebulous waffle which too often fills the slot and makes David Coomes 'hit the roof'. It is the *Today* 'Saturday Essay', a four and a half minute slice of unmediated argument from a distinctly different and entirely secular perspective. Liddle explains the thinking behind it.

'The "Saturday Essay" is an attempt to get good quality writing on to the *Today* programme from sources not constrained by the things *Today* interviewees are usually constrained by. We have a procession of politicians who are all constrained by their political parties – now that Alan Clark is dead! Even the university academics, they all have, to some degree, to watch what they say.' Saturday essayists don't.

Liddle says he decided to challenge consensus thinking, to air views that some of his audience certainly share but rarely hear expressed in mainstream debate. 'We wanted truly independent, cantankerous, lateral thinking from talented writers. People who would make listeners think, "My God, I didn't know you could think about it that way."' The original aspiration of persuading Nobel Prize winning authors to contribute proved hard to sustain – Liddle ruing 'the amount of time it took to set up Milan Kundera live from Paris'. So he approached two writers from opposite ends of the political and cultural spectrum, Will Self and Frederick Forsyth. 'Oddly enough,' he muses, 'it's most unpopular with the liberal left, which is increasingly illiberal. They don't merely disagree with what Freddy Forsyth says, they want him stopped from saying it constitutionally because (as far as they are concerned) the BBC should not be doing this. I find that ludicrous.'

Liddle admits his is not a consensual approach. He believes that *Today* should increase its use of unmediated argument and aim for the same clear distinction between hard news and provocative opinion that fills the pages of broadsheet newspapers. 'There's a sort of perversity in me that says the more people balk and complain the more we should pursue that agenda. We should be about difficult things, thinking the unthinkable occasionally.'

David Coomes is the first to accept that society has changed a great deal since the days of 'Lift up your Hearts', that naked appeal to Christian piety, broadcast on the old Home Service from which 'Thought for the Day' can trace its origins. He advises potential contributors to 'remember Britain is no longer a Christian country' and warns them that '"Thought" is just a thought – it certainly isn't meant to be a sermon. You're not trying to change anyone's opinion.'

He also acknowledges that 'Thought for the Day' is not the explanation for *Today*'s peak audience ratings – 'but we don't seem to be turning the listeners off because we're there'.

My own view is that 'Thought for the Day' is flawed. While I don't share Polly Toynbee's outright contempt, I think she identifies a problem that Christina Odone and Jonathan Sacks refuse to confront because their own contributions are so much better than most – that many contributions to 'Thought for the Day' are simply not as good as the journalism which surrounds them. For every inspired, provocative or simply charming

'Thought' there are five that do not begin to pass muster. I suspect its popularity depends upon the fact that it marks a change in the sometimes relentless pace of the *Today* programme. As for the nameless producer's recommendation of it as the ideal time for a cup of coffee – millions of Britons make tea or coffee at just that time of the morning. A fair proportion clearly enjoy listening to something more relaxing than a bruising confrontation between John Humphrys and a cabinet minister while they drink it. But the same effect could be achieved with a daily poem, a reading from literature or a daily essay. Every other item on *Today* earns its place on journalistic merit. 'Thought' does not. The audience will never know how much more usefully the time could be used until the BBC has the courage to experiment. There would be howls of protest but I doubt a single listener would abandon the programme. It is an old adage in radio that you can never be sure what the listeners will enjoy until you have let them hear it.

EIGHT

Today *and Spin*

———

The best evidence that *Today* is the political agenda-setter it claims to be is the behaviour of politicians and the people who serve them. To those who question whether one early morning news programme, broadcast on the unfashionable medium of radio, can really be more powerful than newspaper, television and internet outlets combined, the programme's most prominent guests have a clear answer. They think it is, and their treatment of it reflects that conviction.

'It is one of the main daily agenda-setters,' says the former Chairman of the Conservative Party, Sir Michael Ancram, 'because those who follow on during the media day tend to take their lead from the *Today* programme.' Ancram himself, on occasion a fierce critic of the BBC's political coverage, admits that he listens to the programme 'invariably. It's stimulating. Sometimes it makes me so angry it wakes me up better than any cup of coffee could.'

That mixture of respect and irritation is shared at the other end of the political spectrum. New Labour's media management strategy before and during the 1997 general election is widely regarded as the most professional operation of its kind ever conducted by a British political party. The *Today* programme was a crucial element in that strategy. Labour insiders say they considered it far more important than any other individual programme or newspaper.

As British politics became a ferocious battle for the centre ground, a development normally attributed to Labour's two-decade struggle to compete with the transformation brought about by four consecutive terms of Conservative government, so the desire to 'control the message' replaced previous wars over the content of party manifestos. With Labour and Conservative politicians united in agreement about core economic and social objectives, the capacity to 'spin' better than one's opponents inevitably became as important as the policy being spun.

The effect on the relationship between *Today* and the political parties was dramatic. Gradually every second of airtime on the programme became a source of contention. If *Today* was the nation's agenda-setter, and there was absolute acceptance that it was, then the media manipulators employed by the parties were ruthlessly determined to ensure that the agenda set was theirs. 'There was a chorus of Party press officers which called *Today* day in, day out,' remembers Frances Halewood, the programme's deputy editor for most of the period between the 1992 and 1997 general elections. 'The targeting by Labour became frenzied. They knew they were in with a real chance of winning the election and they weren't going to let that slip away as they had in 1992.'

This meant agonizing battles over who would appear, for how long, what they would talk about and who they would be interviewed by. In the years leading up to the 1997 general election, New Labour, under the impressive media management of Peter Mandelson, achieved new heights of professionalism and sheer awkwardness in its dealings with the *Today* programme. 'Our view was that in nine cases out of ten a policy initiative had to be launched on *Today*,' says Brian Wilson MP, now a Minister at the Department of Trade and Industry, and in 1997 a senior member of Labour's campaign team. It was the essential launch pad. 'If you had a line that Labour didn't like on the 6.30 a.m. bulletin,' recalls Roger Mosey, *Today*'s editor until shortly before the 1997 election, 'you got called instantly. Often Labour complaints had some substance. That was their cleverness. If there was a glimmer of inaccuracy, they were on to you.'

Brian Wilson agrees that the programme was deliberately targeted: 'The great thing in 1997 was that New Labour was a lean, mean, fighting machine. We deliberately made a concerted effort to get a fair crack of the whip on *Today*, so, yes, we did complain.' But, he maintains, 'I would never say you could bully your way onto the *Today* programme. That was not the way it was done. Complaints lose their value if you voice them too often.'

But New Labour was not always so courteous and correct. It engaged in deliberate, long-term softening-up of the *Today* team. A key player in this process was Tim Allan, then deputy to Alastair Campbell in Tony Blair's personal media team. Allan had a masterful understanding of BBC procedures. He rapidly recognized that a complaint about an individual journalist could result in hours of corporate soul-searching, and that the reporter, producer or presenter concerned would be obliged to justify him or herself in a succession of interviews with BBC managers. The important aspect of this was not the formal response, since the BBC usually defended its staff, but the amount of internal trouble provoked before that was ever issued.

'With the *Today* programme the stakes are high enough,' explained one very senior New Labour insider, 'and were certainly high enough in 1997. That justified our decision to use our understanding of the BBC's civil service mentality to put staff under as much pressure as we could. Our objective was not to make them surrender but to make them exercise self-censorship, to make them think, "Is it really worth provoking New Labour this morning or will I spend my entire weekend defending my decision if I do?"'

Tim Allan used this tactic relentlessly. Some of the producers to whom he spoke by telephone, or about whom he wrote formal letters of complaint to the BBC's head of news and current affairs, describe him as a bully. Several journalists working on *Today* before and during the 1997 election campaign remember Allan as the figure who gave New Labour a reputation for ruthless, and occasionally dishonest, conduct. 'Tim Allan was a zealot,' one former producer recalls. 'At that time everyone in New Labour believed in what they were doing, they were all passionate about victory, but Allan was notorious for taking it all too far.' Senior BBC managers downplay the extent to which journalists were, and still are, subjected to bullying and harassment by New Labour staff. They are peculiarly coy about the period preceding the 1997 election campaign and the conduct of Tim Allan. *Today* staff are more forthright. One former editor has vivid recollections of the occasion on which Allan insulted and harassed a junior producer until forced by the duty editor to apologize and back down.

But for all his single-mindedness, Allan was an amateur when compared to his mentor, Peter Mandelson. 'Tim Allan produced melodrama on the phone,' says Honor Wilson, a *Today* duty editor before and during the 1997 election, 'but Peter Mandelson was much worse.' Wilson remembers a Sunday afternoon in 1996. A minor controversy had arisen in the newspapers over an aspect of Labour policy. The issue itself was so trivial that none of the BBC journalists involved in what followed can remember precisely what it was. They have very precise recollections of the role played by the man who has since been sacked from the Cabinet twice.

Nick Robinson, who had once been the National Chairman of the Young Conservatives, had just joined the BBC as a political correspondent, recalls Honor Wilson, who was editing the programme that day. 'It was about 2.30 in the afternoon. I had just written Nick's name up on the board [a large white notice-board in the old *Today* programme office on which the names of live interviewees were recorded as a basic precaution against booking two guests for the same slot]. Nick was provisionally booked for a 6.30 slot. I hadn't finally decided we would do him, but it was a relatively quiet day. It was one in the bag.'

At this point Peter Mandelson called. 'He insisted on knowing if we were planning to interview Nick Robinson,' Wilson says. 'He seemed very confident that he had every right to know what was going to be on the programme. I said I had not decided and that it was a matter for me. Mandelson was adamant. He said, "You have to take Robinson off. He is a Tory. He is biased. He is a Conservative sympathiser." I am certain that he used all of those phrases.' When Wilson refused to back down, insisting that the Labour Party had no authority to dictate the content of her running order, Mandelson argued that *Today* was guilty of relentless and deliberate anti-Labour bias.

'I was genuinely astonished by the detailed knowledge Mandelson had of *Today* programme running orders,' comments Wilson. 'He knew exactly what had been on the programme for the previous fortnight. His argument was that the programme had shown a consistent pattern of bias against the Labour Party. As far as he was concerned, Nick Robinson was part of that pattern. He seemed absolutely certain that he could simply tell me not to put Robinson on the programme and that I would obey him. He became extremely rude and abusive when I did not accept his point of view. He called me "stupid" on three occasions. I was "incredibly stupid" not to accept that what I was planning to do was wrong. Mandelson told me that John Birt [the Director General of the BBC] was a close personal friend. He made it clear that he could get me sacked. He said that if I did not do as he instructed, he could ensure that I was never promoted at the *Today* programme. He reminded me again of his "close friendship" with the Director General, that getting me dismissed or ruining my career would not be difficult for him.'

Peter Mandelson's telephone conversation with Honor Wilson lasted for nearly an hour. Before the politician hung up in disgust at not getting his own way, Wilson asked him how he would characterize their conversation. He described it as 'a conversation between colleagues'. Honor Wilson told him she had never had a conversation like that with a colleague. Indeed, she told him that it was 'the most abusive, confrontational and blatantly offensive' conversation she had experienced in her career as a journalist. Mandelson appeared quite taken aback.

Putting the phone down, she announced to the *Today* team – who had been transfixed by this outbreak of war by telephone – 'Well, we have to run Nick Robinson now. Even if we put him on to discuss what he did in his garden on Sunday, we have to do Nick Robinson.' Wilson remembered a column she had read in the *Guardian* newspaper, describing how, with a combination of forensic intellect, bullying language and naked threats, Peter Mandelson had reduced its author to tears. 'That's what he wanted to do to me,' thought Wilson. 'He wanted to reduce me to tears.'

But bullying of that nature was not the worst weapon in New Labour's armoury. 'In a way that was the routine bit,' says another *Today* staffer. 'Mandelson and Tim Allan both swore at people and very occasionally we swore back. It was fairly straightforward and pretty juvenile. The bigger problem was their habit of writing poisonous letters of complaint to the head of News and Current Affairs or the Director General. They would select an individual producer or duty editor, concoct an absurdly selective version of a telephone conversation they had conducted with that person, add an additional element of pure malice and guarantee that the victim had a hellish time explaining himself to his managers.'

According to those who experienced it, Tim Allan was the master of this tactic. He knew how hard it is for anyone to defend themselves against a fictitious allegation. 'Tim Allan made a formal complaint about me to the BBC's head of News and Current Affairs,' recalls this anonymous staffer who went on to become a senior newspaper executive on a pro-Labour broadsheet. 'It was complete nonsense. I had requested an interview with Tony Blair on a topic I knew he was unlikely to discuss. The answer was no. I was not surprised. Forty-eight hours later I discovered that Allan had written to Tony Hall [then the BBC's head of News and Current Affairs] accusing me of unprofessional conduct and deliberately misleading him in order to obtain an interview with Blair. It should have been funny. Blair had never even contemplated appearing. But that didn't seem to matter to Allan. He knew he could tie another journalist up in BBC bureaucracy. He knew he could waste hours of my time by forcing me to prepare denials of events which had simply never occurred. I hand it to him. He knew how the BBC operated and it was an effective tactic. Next time I wanted to make a bid for a senior Labour politician to discuss a sensitive subject, I certainly thought about how my invitation might be misrepresented.'

Has such political pressure diminished since the 1997 general election? 'No,' says Rod Liddle, editor of *Today* since 1998. 'We still get that every day. But they've become a bit wiser… in that they're far more likely to contact the very top of the Corporation. They know it is, to some degree at least, motivated by fear. You send your letter to Greg Dyke, then you know it's going to be taken very seriously indeed and a vast committee of people will start ringing their hands over it. The civil service mentality at the BBC,' he adds, 'is such that … the imperative is always to be cautious and not to fuck up, and it militates against good journalism. I think it probably also means we apologize probably rather more than we should.'

Liddle, the most forthright, least corporate editor *Today* has ever had, insists that the BBC creates burdens for its own staff by behaving in this way. 'They've got to understand they're not dealing with the general public. That's the way you deal with an ordinary member of the public who is upset by something he's heard. When Alastair Campbell writes a letter, which he does once a week at least, either to me or to the head of News and Current Affairs, and makes a number of points and insists, "This is outrageous journalism on the *Today* programme. It's appalling!" he's trying to make a party political point.' Liddle believes the Corporation's standard response to men like Campbell should be to say, 'No, Alastair. You are wrong. The stuff was fine.'

But attempts by political parties to try and influence the *Today Programme*'s agenda by fair means or foul go further back. There was the legendary occasion in 1988 when Margaret Thatcher telephoned the programme and asked if she could appear on it. The date was 8 December 1988. Radio Four's 6.00 a.m. news bulletin had informed Britain about the devastating earthquake which had hit Yerevan in the then Soviet republic of Armenia. Thatcher had heard the news and a subsequent interview, broadcast on *Today* at 6.33 a.m., in which the Soviet foreign affairs spokesman, Gennady Gerasimov, told John Humphrys that President Mikhail Gorbachev was no longer coming on a scheduled visit to London. The earthquake, in which 25,000 people had died, required him to remain at home.

Thatcher instructed the press officer on duty at Downing Street to call *Today* and get her on the programme. The studio producer that morning was Roger Fraser. 'When she got through to the cubicle she was charming,' he says. 'I just said, "Yes, Prime Minister" and put her on air immediately.' Thatcher was duly interviewed by John Humphrys, expressed her sympathies for the Armenian people and made it clear that Mikhail Gorbachev had made the right decision: 'When there's trouble like that, home is the place to be.' 'But it was obvious why she'd called,' says Fraser. 'She didn't want the audience to think she didn't know about the earthquake, and definitely didn't want anyone to make too much of the fact that Gorbachev hadn't called her to make his apologies.'

But that was not the end of it. Shortly afterwards, Peter

Mandelson called the *Today* office, already rehearsing the tactics he would later perfect. Frances Halewood was the day editor that morning. 'He was furious, and demanded to know why we had put the Prime Minister on air without asking her any tough questions about domestic politics.' Irritated, Halewood told Mandelson he was being 'conspiratorial and paranoid'. Mrs Thatcher was the Prime Minister. 'Mandelson then called the Director General. He demanded my dismissal.' The surprise is not that Margaret Thatcher listened to the *Today* programme – every senior politician except John Major has done that. The revealing thing was the degree of paranoia occasioned by the appearance of an opponent. Peter Mandelson, then working as Neil Kinnock's top media advisor, had clearly convinced himself that Kinnock deserved to be interviewed too – though Gorbachev was not scheduled to visit the leader of the opposition and Gerasimov had made no reference to the Labour Party.

It was standard political conduct at the time – demanding balance where it already existed and insisting on the right to reply when no criticism had been uttered. 'Norman Tebbit demanded my resignation not long afterwards,' remembers Halewood with wry amusement. Brian Redhead had described the plotters of an abortive coup against Russia's President Gorbachev as 'nasty right-wingers' (nasty left-wingers might have been more appropriate). Halewood refused to correct the reference, insisting that Redhead had not cast aspersions on the British right and had certainly not intended to characterize the orthodox communists who tried to topple Gorbachev as representatives of the Conservative Party. Tebbit was incensed and took his complaint further up the BBC hierarchy.

During this period between the 1987 and 1992 elections Halewood remembers that the Conservative Party often seemed obsessed with the notion that *Today* was biased towards the left. The Conservative peer and *News of the World* columnist Woodrow Wyatt made a conspicuously infantile attempt to prove the theory by faxing the editor and demanding to know how each member of the *Today* team had voted in recent general elections. Nobody had the least intention of telling him: it would have been impossible because the information did not exist and it would have been an extraordinary breach of civil liberties to attempt to obtain it. But Frances Halewood remembers being tempted to tell Wyatt his own political history. At the time the BBC man had voted for all three major political parties. He later went on to work as a media adviser to the Conservative Party.

Woodrow Wyatt was not a serious threat. But Phil Harding, editor of *Today* between 1987 and 1992, remembers the period as one in which pressure from the Conservatives was intense and *Today* stood accused of systematic left-wing bias. The programme was denounced from the platform at Conservative Party conferences and a concerted effort was made to stigmatize Brian Redhead as a dangerous left-winger and active supporter of the Labour Party. 'It started with an article in the *Daily Express* about the *Today* programme and its bias – about something called the Media Monitoring Unit, and it just escalated from there on. At the end of all this I got a book of press cuttings which must have been about 350 or 400 pages.'

This was not the first time *Today* had come under attack from the Conservatives. There had been a very sticky moment in March 1987, shortly before he became editor of the programme, when Brian Redhead clashed with the Chancellor of the Exchequer, Nigel Lawson. It was the morning after the Budget and Redhead had started the showpiece 8.10 interview with typical aplomb: 'Now, what are we to make of the Budget? It appeared to be a Budget rather like the housemaid's baby – only a little one and Prudence, they say, is her name. Well, the father of the child is in our radio car. Mr Lawson, good morning.'

It was typical Redhead. Cheeky. Stylish. Calculated to provoke – but clearly not an ideological statement of any kind. Things deteriorated. Redhead played devil's advocate, alternately suggesting that Lawson might have cut tax more and made a more substantial increase in public spending.

The crunch came on the vexed topic of mass unemployment. Lawson asserted that 'the economy is stronger than it's been at any time since the war and this Budget will ensure that it keeps on'. Redhead pointed out that there were more than 3 million registered unemployed. Lawson retorted that unemployment was falling and that 'as a result of the strength of the economy, unemployment will go on falling throughout the course of this year'. Redhead pointed out that much of the decline in unemployment was due to 'special measures' and quoted the Shadow Chancellor, Roy Hattersely, who had alleged that government job creation schemes involved 'young people being invited to job clubs to play games under the supervision of nursery school teachers'. 'These aren't the real jobs that you used to talk about way back in 1979 and 1980?' concluded the ever-pugnacious Redhead.

Listening to that interview again now, it is obvious that Redhead's statement was interrogative. He was inviting Lawson to deny that the government was engineering a synthetic decrease in the unemployment figures. But Lawson did not interpret it that way. 'Well,' he shot back irritably, 'you've been a supporter of the Labour Party all your life, Brian, so I expect you to say something like that.'

Redhead was calm but palpably furious. To an audience somewhere in the region of 3 million, he declared icily, 'Do you think we should have a one-minute silence now in this interview. One for you to apologize for daring to suggest that you know how I vote, and secondly, perhaps in memory of monetarism, which you have now discarded?'

Lawson saw no cause for a minute's silence. He had simply articulated what was Conservative orthodoxy of the time. The BBC was a nest of whinging lefties dedicated to the overthrow of an elected and massively popular government. Brian Redhead was the leading representative of a cabal committed to the defeat of Thatcherism and all its works. In the circles in which he moved, the Chancellor's comment was regarded as a luminous truth. Redhead was a socialist, wasn't he? Everyone thought so!

Lawson was wrong. Redhead was not a Labour supporter. Nor was he a Conservative. He later revealed that, during the Thatcher years, he had cast his ballot in favour of Nicholas Winterton, a Conservative with impressive right-wing credentials, not because he was a Tory but because he liked and admired Winterton.

'Did I think that Brian showed a systematic bias against the Conservative Party?' ponders Phil Harding. 'No, I don't think he did. I think he did probably have a set of beliefs but they didn't fit into any particular political mould. I think he enjoyed treading on corns. He was just the high profile presenter and I think they picked on him because he was the highest profile presenter. After he died they tended to go for John [Humphrys]. I think they'll go for whoever they think is the highest profile political face, and I don't say that about the Conservative Party alone.'

But the spat with Lawson marked the beginning of the end of the phoney war between the government and the *Today* programme. Until the 1987 general election, Conservative Central Office had been critical, but with a third successive election victory under their belt, and in alliance with sympathetic newspapers and magazines, it adopted a more clinical approach to its allegations that *Today* was biased. 'I don't think I had ever come across anything that sustained,' says Phil Harding. 'The pressure did surprise me and so did the extent of it. It went on for weeks.'

The attacks on bias were appearing in every newspaper in the land. Ideologically sympathetic journalists on newspapers like the *Daily Mail*, *Daily Telegraph* and *Daily Express* were enthusiastically championing the Conservative cause. Around the country Conservative MPs speaking at constituency association dinners could be certain of a round of applause if they mentioned the 'bearded-leftie Redhead' or called *Today* 'biased and vile'. Norman Tebbit and Peter Lilley were famed for their party-piece hostility. But, in private – it is something that emerges again and again in the relationship between the *Today* programme and political parties – cabinet ministers remained absolutely charming about the programme. 'That was the ironic thing about it, because all the time it was going on, the Cabinet was still trooping in and appearing on the programme in large numbers.' During private conversations, senior conservatives were relentlessly charming. Even Norman Tebbit, a man whose private charm has always surprised those who knew him only by reputation, was the perfect gentleman when he found himself in the company of the *Today* programme's editor. 'It was entirely conducted in the press,' says Harding. 'And, interestingly, several cabinet ministers at that point told me privately not to take the slightest bit of notice.'

Of the basic allegation that *Today*'s interviewing and story selection was biased against the government, Harding is dismissive. 'Although I don't think we knew it at the time, when you look back, it's during the post-1988 era that Thatcherism began to unravel. And that was when the pressure was at its highest. There was always a close correlation between the level of unpopularity of the government and the level of complaint about the programme.'

Harding's successor, Roger Mosey, who took control shortly after the 1992 general election, remembers *Today*'s task made easier by the spectacular lack of discipline among Conservative politicians. 'You could get cabinet ministers to pursue their own agenda. The Downing Street machine was completely ill disciplined. We had times when we knew that the reason Ken Clarke was appearing on the programme was because he'd been annoyed by what Michael Howard had said the day before. If you really wanted to get a particular minister on *Today*, you simply put Theresa Gorman [the outspoken Eurosceptic Conservative MP for Billericay] on at ten past seven making Theresa Gorman-type allegations and they immediately responded to it. I had occasions when I had twelve or fourteen Conservatives on the programme in one morning, with no opposition comment at all.'

Mosey insists this was not unbalanced coverage of politics. The Conservatives were not agreeing with each other – indeed, they often inflicted more grievous political wounds on their own colleagues than Labour politicians could have. It was more a question of *Today* providing the forum in which internal schisms in the ruling party could be advertised to the wider electorate. 'You had a government that was falling apart live on your airwaves. And while *Today* must always be about a lot more than just politics that was entertaining, it was good theatre.'

The sense of a government in crisis indulging in daily self-flagellation on the *Today* programme confirmed the suspicions of many grass roots Conservatives that the BBC in general and *Today* in particular was out to get them. But there is a more significant reason for the difference between Conservative handling of *Today* and the approach adopted by New Labour.

Conservatives sincerely believe that the programme is biased against them. 'It has always had a left leaning,' Michael Ancram insists, 'frequently in its presenters but almost exclusively in its producers and editors. And as it is the editors who shape the programme the night before, they have a distinct effect on the political balance of the programme the next day. You can get a *Today* programme on a Monday morning where you have four or five ministers on in a row and not a single opposition spokesman, and not because there isn't an opposition spokesman but because the opposition have not been invited to go on... . So they are actually able to create a raw party-political broadcast. *Today*'s argument is that their interviewers will make sure these government ministers are tested. I have to say that in some cases that doesn't happen.'

His predecessors were certain that Brian Redhead was actively hostile to Conservatism. Modern Conservatives feel equally strongly about Jim Naughtie. 'I think Jim Naughtie has a natural aversion to the Conservative Party,' says Michael Ancram. 'He is most likely to let his slip show. The timbre of contempt in the voice can often carry a message in itself as opposed to the rather light, deferential tone of voice used when a government minister is on. And that's nothing to do with the questions. It's to do with the style and the tone.'

Before their defeat in the 2001 election, Ancram and his colleagues at Conservative Central Office were equally critical of *Today*'s editor, Rod Liddle. Liddle has never hidden the fact that, while an undergraduate at the LSE, he worked as a research assistant and press officer to Labour's Shadow Cabinet. Liddle, and the BBC, insist that he is a professional journalist who leaves any personal beliefs at home when he goes to work. Michael Ancram insists that in his opinion, 'there has been a tendency on the *Today* programme ... to allow that distinctive political inclination to show through in the way that the programme is produced'.

Roger Mosey is emphatic, however. 'I can't remember a single case when we compromised the journalism. But there are things we've learned over the years. A lot of press officers used to call the studio while the programme was on air. That's the way the Westminster Village works. They would say, "I demand to be put through to the programme editor!" and, in the old days, sometimes those calls got through. If you're trying to edit the programme and trying to talk to the presenter and everyone else and you've got someone shouting in your ear, it is a lot of pressure. Our staff now have instructions that they can say they won't take those calls.'

The early 1980s to the mid-1990s mark was, in Rod Liddle's assessment, the period when the *Today* programme was most politically obsessed: 'a very febrile political atmosphere – a majority of one for quite a lot of that time – in which almost anything which you did politically could bring the government down ... [a] wonderful era when politicians would come onto the *Today* programme to make policy and to change policy overnight. But they hadn't yet got to the stage that they were scared shitless of what would happen to them by coming onto the *Today* programme.'

The advent of Tony Blair's government in 1997 brought abrupt change. Now, says Liddle, ministers very rarely make policy on the *Today* programme, 'and increasingly you find that, when they've been guilty of some form of wickedness or incompetence, it's not the *Today* programme that usually gets the first interview. It's usually one of the softer, patsier places such as *Breakfast with Frost* or *GMTV*. So they wised up. It's now totally controlled and there's very few politicians who will step outside that control and speak from the heart.'

There are powerful suspicions indeed at the BBC that Labour in government has worked hard to reduce the significance of one challenging, agenda-setting programme. Alastair Campbell was allegedly quoted as saying, 'I would like to destroy the Radio Four sequences, that's my first task' – by which he would clearly have meant the *Today* programme and the *World at One*. 'How did they do that?' asks Rod Liddle. 'Well, you had Tony Blair saying that he never listened to it. He said soon after taking office, "I listen to *GMTV* in the morning." (Incidentally, he also said he doesn't read the newspapers.)' The New Labour strategy appears to have found expression in December 1997, when a bitter argument exploded between programme and party. The pretext was an interview between John Humphrys and the Social Security Secretary, Harriet Harman.

The government was under considerable pressure from its own backbenches over its proposal to cut the benefit entitlement of single parents. The Prime Minister himself had been obliged to appear at the despatch box to defend the policy, which appeared neo-Thatcherite to many of his usually loyal supporters. Harman got the job of defending the cuts on the *Today* programme.

The interview lasted approximately eight minutes. Harman sounded nervous and insecure. Humphrys made no concessions. He repeatedly interrupted the minister, doing his best to keep her focused on the issue in question. Harman was openly evasive. 'If you cut something,' Humphrys suggested to her at one point, 'you make somebody worse off. It's a fact.' Not a fact Ms Harman was willing to concede, so Humphrys tried again. 'This is Alice in Wonderland stuff, isn't it?' he suggested, and, 'with the greatest respect, you're answering the wrong question'.

The presenter had employed similar persistence with Conservative ministers in the previous regime. Some had been angered, though Kenneth Clarke, the most high profile of Humphrys' Tory victims, consistently refused to complain. Harman, or her advisers at Millbank Tower, took a less tolerant stance. In opposition the Labour Party had revelled in the forensic evisceration of Conservative ministers by *Today* presenters. That did not mean it expected to receive the same treatment now that Labour politicians had taken possession of the red boxes and ministerial cars.

Labour's Director of Communications, David Hill, fired off a furious letter to the *Today* editor, Jon Barton. Concentrating his fire on the presenter, the Labour man wrote that the 'John Humphrys problem' had 'assumed new proportions'. 'We need to talk now,' he insisted, 'as this is serious', and revealed that Labour 'is now considering whether, as a party, we will suspend co-operation [with the *Today* programme]. ... Individual government departments will continue to make their own minds up, but we will now give very careful thought to any bid to us in order to make absolutely sure that your listeners are not going to be subjected to a repeat of the ridiculous exchange.'

It was naked political bullying, and Barton's response was robust. 'I thought,' he wrote, 'it was one of the best attempts yet to establish why Labour has decided to cut benefits to lone parents.' As is usually the case with controversy about the *Today* programme, the newspapers lapped it up. 'Labour has declared war on BBC Radio's Today Programme', wrote the *Independent*.

In early 1998 Alastair Campbell made it plain that the gloves were off. At a Downing Street briefing he described the BBC as a 'downmarket, dumbed-down, over-staffed, over-bureaucratic, ridiculous organization'. But though the belligerent attitude of New Labour's spin doctors might suggest that they really do hold a programme like *Today* in low regard, the truth is that, understanding the unique power of the show, they want to control it. Another powerful manifestation of the 'if you're not with us, you're against us' philosophy was Labour's vigorous attempt to influence the BBC's selection of a replacement for Jon Barton at *Today*.

One of the front runners for the job Rod Liddle eventually won was Kevin Marsh, editor of the *World at One* since 1992 and a formidable political journalist – and patently far too open-minded to be compliant with the Labour Party machine. In October 1997 a Labour source made a spiteful telephone call to the *Observer* accusing Marsh of conducting 'something of a vendetta' against the government. The Prime Minister's press secretary, Alastair Campbell, followed up with a lengthy letter to Richard Clemmow, then head of BBC News Programmes, alleging that Marsh was 'closed to reason' and guilty of peddling an 'anti-Labour follow-any-old-Tory-guff agenda'. With Marsh's candidature now highly controversial, Liddle – who was as well suited to the task as the man from *World at One* – was appointed. The BBC followed its own procedures to the letter, but there are senior figures in the Labour government who believe their intervention was decisive. They did not want Kevin Marsh to run the *Today* programme and he was not chosen. That, in New Labour speak, was a result.

Rod Liddle is confident that, since those immediate post-election months, government – and indeed opposition – politicians have learned the error of their ways. Their experiments with interviews on *Frost*, Five Live, *GMTV* and local radio achieved, he acknowledges, half of their objective: it allowed them to speak directly to their target audiences without the intercession of a challenging and well-briefed presenter. But there was a vital element missing. Recognition of the problem, says Liddle, has pushed politicians back towards *Today*, where he wants them. 'They missed the newspaper audience which inevitably came as a result of being asked interesting questions.' Tony Blair, for example, talked to *Today* six times within a year.

But Liddle nevertheless acknowledges a key change in the relationship between *Today* and the political establishment. 'There certainly seems to be no feeling of obligation – that, "Oh, Christ, we ought to do the *Today* programme." You know, something important came up and [politicians] thought, "This ought to be in the public domain. I ought to be on the main programme talking about it." I think that's gone completely. I don't think anyone feels an obligation any more to talk to anyone. Their sole wish is to manage the crisis, and there seems to be no sense of public service in being seen to answer tough questions about it. I don't think anybody does that any more. That makes it difficult for the *Today* programme because, of course, that's where we get our bread and butter. Which is why, two or three years ago, we changed focus. We still do the big political interviews when we get them. We still do a lot of political debate. But what we decided we had to do is original journalism ourselves, at reporter level, and break stories and preferably do it every single day. And then, off the back of that, we try to bring ministers to account. It's a big challenge.'

The truth remains that *Today* is worth spinning, worth lambasting, because it has the capacity to define which issues are worthy of debate. The constant allegations of bias made against the programme demonstrate the central position it occupies in British political life. Comments made on the *Today* programme are heard by a huge audience of opinion formers. Whenever you hear a politician say that *Today* no longer matters as much as it once did, bear this in mind. Politicians may well want it to be true. This is probably the best available evidence that it is not.

Today's *Dilemma*

S ince the introduction of digital broadcasting, and the growth
of twenty-four hour radio and television news channels, it
has become fashionable in some political, journalistic and media
studies circles to argue that the power of *Today* has diminished.
Among the most active proponents of this view are senior BBC
journalists and executives. Some of them have a vested interest in
denigrating established programmes. Their careers depend on the
success of new projects.

The first serious assault on *Today*'s pre-eminence emerged
out of an experiment conducted during the Gulf War of 1991.
Jenny Abramsky, then in charge of radio news and current
affairs, had long nurtured an ambition to launch a rolling news
station. Twenty-four hour radio news was already a reality in
the United States and in France. Abramsky and a few forward-
looking colleagues saw no reason why it should not succeed in
Britain.

In common with senior colleagues, opposition politicians and
journalists Abramsky recognized that the BBC's coverage of the
Falklands War had been less than entirely objective. It had been
exceptionally hard to reflect the Argentine perspective. Military
and civil service press officers had exercised near total control
over the flow of information. Robert Fox, who travelled to the
Falklands with the British task force ordered to recapture the
islands, was the first reporter to set foot on the Falklands after
liberation. 'It is very difficult,' he said in an interview on *Today*
on 16 June 1982, 'because there is this temptation just to become
part of a propaganda machine. It is very hard to be critical given
the very strict kind of censorship we have from the Ministry of
Defence... . There is a military officer who goes through one's
copy just to make sure that no secrets are divulged.'

Censorship during the Falklands campaign was not perfect. On several occasions the Ministry of Defence in London seemed not to know what its staff in the combat zone were doing. Just before the 2nd Battalion of the Parachute Regiment attacked Goose Green, their position was revealed by the BBC acting on information released by the MOD in London. The attack was almost called off as the Argentines moved in reinforcements by helicopter.

Nevertheless, censorship reduced the objectivity of news broadcasting. Jenny Abramsky regarded the new conflict between Iraq and the Allies as an opportunity to develop new rules for the coverage of a war in which British lives were at risk. It was also a golden opportunity to experiment with non-stop radio news coverage. Abramsky's wartime rolling news channel was not Radio Five Live. It was broadcast on one of Radio Four's frequencies, and included all the existing Radio Four sequence programmes, *Today*, *World at One*, *PM* and *World Tonight*. It was thrown together at the last minute and put enormous pressure on everyone who volunteered to contribute. Some of the journalists who travelled to the Middle East to cover the war came to refer to the temporary news channel as 'Mother of All Battles Radio' (in truth, the name of the channel used by Saddam Hussein to broadcast wartime propaganda and religious homilies to the Iraqi people) or just 'Rolling Bollocks'.

But the format worked. A new generation of neo-Thatcherite BBC managers regarded it as an exercise in squeezing more work out of existing staff, but journalists like Abramsky took a more enlightened view. It proved there was an audience for broadcast news at all hours of day and night. True, interest had been maximized by the sheer drama of war, and the BBC had spent unprecedented sums to ensure that every theatre of conflict was covered by staff correspondents. There were journalists in Baghdad, Israel, Saudi Arabia and Jordan, reporters on aircraft carriers in the Gulf and accompanying ground forces on the Saudi/Kuwaiti border. News briefings in Washington, DC, London and at Desert Storm headquarters in Saudi Arabia filled large chunks of airtime. But the principle was established. Non-stop news had been attempted and it had worked.

After the war, it soon emerged that Abramsky was keen to

launch a permanent version of the rolling news format. Colleagues assumed the new channel would follow the Gulf War
pattern. It would be highbrow, Radio Four-style broadcasting,
filling the gaps between established programmes like *Today*.
Nobody imagined what followed. In 1993 Abramsky announced
plans for a twenty-four hour news and sport channel wholly separate from Radio Four. Five Live would not include the great
flagships like *Today* and *World at One*. It would be broadcast on
an entirely separate medium-wave frequency and it would produce its own programmes to compete head to head with everything on Radio Four.

The desire for rolling news had been combined with the
BBC's ambition to attract a younger audience throughout the
United Kingdom. For all its popularity and success, Radio Four
failed the test of universal appeal. It was favoured by middle-
aged professionals resident in the English Home Counties, that
ill-defined group routinely referred to as the British Establishment and their supporters. Five Live would be 'an airship float-
ing above the nation', a station for the whole country, livelier,
less pompous and more attractive to younger non-establishment
licence-fee payers.

The decision caused outrage among many *Today* programme
staff. While a lot of the journalists who launched Five Live and
made it work were recruited from the ranks of *Today* (among
them several of the new station's original presenters, including
Diana Madill, a *Today* reporter whose Five Live programme
defeated *Today* to win the 1995 Sony Radio Award for Best
Response to a News Event), others stayed behind, determined to
sabotage the launch of the upstart station.

One policy above all others provoked seething fury. Shortly
prior to Five Live's launch in March 1994, BBC News and Current Affairs declared a policy of 'News Priority'. What it meant
was quite simple: BBC correspondents and reporters working
for domestic (i.e. non-World Service) outlets, no matter where
they were in the world, would offer breaking news to Five Live
first. Henceforth the first interview or news report on a fresh
story would appear on the rolling news station, even if it was
taking place while the *Today* programme was actually on air.

Today staff were appalled. It was the end of *Today*'s

previously unchallenged role as the programme that was always first with the news. There are many senior figures at the BBC and beyond who regard the launch of Five Live as the beginning of a process which has diminished *Today*. When Five Live was launched, Roger Mosey, editor of the *Today* programme between 1992 and 1996, remembers meeting a newspaper media editor who warned him that his audience would be cut in half. It wasn't, but Mosey, now head of BBC television news, has become a reluctant convert to the ranks of the modernizing cabal which insists that broadcasting is now too diverse for *Today* to retain its influence. 'There's more media noise these days,' says Mosey. 'It's harder for the *Today* programme to be the undivided focus of attention. My guess is that that in television news five, ten or fifteen years ago, the *Today* programme was the thing that everyone had heard, whereas now we do get people who have listened to Five Live or *GMTV* or Sky. I think it was David Hill [the Labour Party's former director of communications] who said at the time of the 1997 election that as far as the Westminster Village was concerned, and the Shadow Cabinet as it then was, the *Today* programme was the be all and end all. Whereas the people they were hiring to run their media monitoring unit were the sort of bright twenty-five year olds who listened to Jazz FM or ITN News Channel or Sky. They couldn't quite get why everyone else was so focused on this one show.'

'*Today* is less important than it was as a means of breaking stories,' agrees a senior Conservative spin doctor who insists on anonymity. 'It's worth using to brief opinion-formers but *Today* is no longer a voter-reach medium. It is listened to by an audience of approximately 1 million politically committed people. *GMTV* is watched by 3 million non-committed voters. As a result, the Prime Minister hardly ever uses it now. *Today* no longer sets newspaper agendas. There used to be a thirty-six hour news cycle. Not now – these days, twenty-four hours feels like a very long news cycle. Now the truth is that *Today* follows the newspapers.' In spite of this, maintains the source, '*Today* is incredibly self-important. It can't believe that it doesn't matter any more. *Today* staff can't believe that we would deliberately ignore them, deliberately schedule them out of our plans, but we have and we do.' This description of deliberate scheduling out was a direct and intentional reference to the Conservative leader William Hague's decision not to appear on *Today* during the 2000 Conservative Party conference.

Another development, now deliberately forgotten by the BBC managers who once sought to enforce it, was the keen desire of former Director General John Birt to cut costs and exercise central control by homogenizing BBC news. That campaign reached its zenith in late September 1997 when Birt sent his messengers, Richard Clemmow (then head of BBC News Programmes) and Stephen Mitchell (then deputy head of News Programmes) to inform *Today* staff of a frankly demented decision to reorganize BBC News and Current Affairs.

The Birt strategy involved the imposition of a tier of five 'executive editors' over the heads of individual programme editors. Clemmow and Mitchell outlined the idea to a meeting of seventy journalists, including John Humphrys, Jim Naughtie and Sue MacGregor, in the *Today* office. Accustomed to staff resentment of Birt's management style and philosophy, neither Clemmow nor Mitchell can have expected an enthusiastic response. They certainly did not anticipate outright mutiny. Having sent Clemmow and Mitchell packing with an entire camel-load of fleas in their ears, the *Today* presenters, backed by their radio colleagues Robin Lustig, James Cox, Nick Clarke and Chris Lowe, followed up with a letter. 'You say you are not seeking homogeneity,' they wrote, such vigorous argument reflecting a confidence that their high public profile rendered them relatively immune from reprisals, 'but it is beyond us to understand how a single commission team across all programmes could possibly provide the richness and variety of material that the programmes generate at present. We all believe it is simply impossible to maintain programmes in their present form without their own dedicated teams and editors.'

The rebellion soon spread. Jeremy Paxman interrupted a sabbatical to deride the whole idea as an attempt to turn BBC News into 'a sausage-machine'. The Labour MP Austin Mitchell, a former BBC journalist, accused the Director General of attempting to force 'all the news into a Birtian Kenwood mixer'. The critics knew all too well what was really going on. With the licence fee then pegged to inflation-level increases, Birt needed to make 30 per cent cuts from existing news and current affairs programmes in order to finance BBC News 24 (launched in November 1997) and other experiments in digital broadcasting. *Today*, with its elitist reputation and treasured individuality, was targeted because it did not adhere to his 'one size fits all' approach. The plan backfired badly, and the *Today*-inspired rebellion marked the high-water mark of Birtian reform. Cuts were still imposed but the 'executive editors' strategy was diluted beyond recognition.

Nevertheless, the Birt regime massively expanded a sub-division of BBC News and Current Affairs called 'Newsgathering'. The theory, in simple terms, was that Newsgathering would deploy the best of the BBC's reporters and correspondents, who would then file reports to a centralized bi-media (radio and television) operation, from which programme editors would select what they wanted. But editors would have little say in deciding which stories and issues the correspondents and reporters would cover. This strategy achieved precisely what John Birt's many critics predicted. Programmes were shorn of their individuality. Key editorial objectives were set centrally. News coverage was characterized by a homogeneity that sometimes threatened to become blandness.

The 1997 landslide victory for a New Labour government represented a yet bigger challenge to *Today*'s former hegemony. In the view of Michael Ancram, the former Chairman of the Conservative Party, *Today*'s editorial agenda underwent dramatic change after the election, with the programme concluding that 'we live in a new dimension where people are not interested in confrontational politics any more. The government is there and we will report the government but forget the rest. And that, I thought, was very unhealthy, and said so to the BBC in no uncertain terms.'

Many senior BBC executives agree that immediately after the Labour Party's victory in 1997, *Today* went badly wrong. The period coincided with the appointment of James Boyle, a former head of BBC Radio Scotland, as the new controller of Radio Four. Former colleagues insist that Boyle was out of his depth in the job, that he did not understand the nature of the Radio Four audience and was guilty of attempting to popularize the channel by introducing low-quality programmes which offended traditional listeners. Boyle's many admirers argue that he was simply doing what the BBC asked him to do: take Radio Four out of its established heartlands and make it relevant to a broader section of the British public.

Boyle certainly made a considerable difference to the *Today* programme. It was extended to begin at 6.00 not 6.30 in the morning. *Yesterday in Parliament*, the daily review of debates in the House of Commons and the House of Lords, was moved to Radio Four's long-wave frequency. This was a trick Boyle had perfected at the infinitely smaller and woefully parochial Radio Scotland. Frequency splitting allowed him to keep the *Today* programme doing what it does best (interviews and reports on news stories) between 8.30 and 9.00 in the morning, while the minority who wanted to hear day old news from the Palace of Westminster could do so by tuning their radios to the long wave frequency.

But although the decision to deprive the majority of *Today* listeners who tune in on FM frequencies of *Yesterday in Parliament* has since turned out to be a very good idea, it did not feel like it at first. Boyle appeared to want *Today* to lead listeners in to the gentler talk-based shows which follow it after the 9.00 a.m. news bulletin, when the audience routinely disappeared. Controllers of Radio Four are acutely aware that *Today* wins more listeners than any other programme broadcast on the station. Many so-called 'Radio Four listeners' listen to very little else.

Today, then under the editorship of Jon Barton (a journalist whose stewardship of the programme is unanimously regarded as a failure), interpreted Boyle's wishes as a licence to broadcast soft, fluffy discussions and features. They did not suit the style of the programme's presenters nor did they reflect the expertise of the production team. It was, as one veteran *Today* producer puts it, 'like chucking half an hour of Blue Peter into the middle of *Newsnight* and wondering why it sounded absurd'. Boyle and Barton, says another former *Today* editor, 'had an obsession with what they called "real people". It meant that instead of interviewing politicians and debating issues with people who participated in the development and implementation of policy, *Today* started interviewing individual teachers about education, social workers about benefits policy, Greenpeace members about the future of the environment. Some of them were very interesting, but on the whole it meant that folk who would never have got more than a fifteen-second sound bite in a package before were being interrogated by John Humphrys or Jim Naughtie. They didn't know enough to handle it. They spoke for themselves, not for a genuine constituency of interest. That sort of thing should be left to local radio. It was a bloody disaster.'

The worst thing about this approach was that it suited the government. Every moment spent covering this softer agenda was a moment not spent interviewing the opposition. *Today* staff, including Rod Liddle, accept that under Barton's editorship *Today* developed a tendency to ignore debate between government and opposition in favour of confronting ministers with individual citizens or pressure groups whose lives or interests were affected by government policy. The Conservative Party regarded this as conclusive proof that *Today* was pro-Blair, an ally of the New Labour project. That was not the intention, but many BBC staff acknowledge that it took *Today* several years to understand that the election of the first Labour government in two decades was not the end of politics as we know it. The private diagnosis at *Today* is of a BBC consensus that the British public had endured enough political controversy. It was time to seek fresh pastures, to cover a broader, less elitist agenda, even if that meant a shift away from the very issues and approaches that had made the programme great.

'James Boyle did not have a clue what he was doing,' says Rod Liddle bluntly. 'The *Today* programme lost a million listeners in a year. I remember James Boyle coming into the newsroom to address the journalists and to offer reassurance. He said we were beginning to fill the troughs. That caused real offence. Filling the troughs? Is that any way to speak about *Today*?'

Boyle's many friends and admirers point out that few of the changes he introduced to Radio Four's schedule have been abandoned since. *Today*'s extended duration has been kept as the audience has returned. Furthermore, they recall that Boyle predicted there would be a decline in audience while his reforms bedded in. Boyle himself agrees that the period after the 1997 general election was difficult for the *Today* programme and for news journalism in general, but says that it was a reflection of the national mood. 'It was very clear that the sense of circus had gone when the Conservative government finally lost office. Right across television and radio there had been memorable confrontations between BBC journalists and conservative politicians. The Labour Party came in and, of course, had decided that wasn't what they were going to do. There was a while when you didn't get the sense of courtroom drama and you could see the numbers slightly trailing off because of that. The editor of *Today* handles the agenda for *Today*. I never made any editorial decisions about the journalism. How could I?'

In 1998 Rod Liddle succeeded Jon Barton as editor of *Today*. Liddle has spectacularly breached an unwritten BBC convention. He has made himself famous. Very few *Today* listeners ever knew what Jenny Abramsky or Phil Harding looked like. They were safely anonymous figures, happy to conceal their personalities and to exercise their influence within the byzantine structures of the BBC.

But everything about Liddle screams flamboyance. His suits, though obviously expensive, are rarely accompanied by ties. His greying hair is worn slightly too long, more in the style of a rock musician. He is almost never without a cigarette (Raffles or something similarly inexpensive), swears constantly and, although not brought up in the capital, affects a working-class south London accent and speaks of BBC mandarins contemptuously as 'wankers', 'prats' or 'fucking Oxbridge clones'. His office walls at BBC television centre are decorated with pictures of semi-naked actresses – specifically, Liddle insists, to infuriate politically correct colleagues. He espouses the values and lifestyles of writers like Will Self, Martin Amis and Julie Burchill. Women are addressed as 'girl' or 'babe'; men, invariably, as 'mate'. He is the first *Today* editor to write a weekly newspaper column, and is happy to tell *Guardian* readers of the occasion on which he nearly set fire to his penis with a cigarette while attempting to smoke, urinate and edit a script simultaneously. An iconoclast who named his first child Wat after Wat Tyler, the leader of the Peasants' Revolt, he wants to be considered mad, bad and dangerous to know.

But the real Liddle is slightly less outrageous than the calculated performance. He is good at creating high-profile ambiguity. He is the anti-establishment radical who has climbed steadily up the BBC hierarchy without seriously blotting his copybook (his change from south London drawl to elegant received pronunciation in the presence of a politician or senior BBC mandarin is extremely funny). He is the former Labour Shadow Cabinet adviser who promoted his own (almost entirely fictional) candidature for the editorship of the relentlessly right-wing *Spectator* magazine. He is scathingly sceptical about the European Union and the single currency but hostile to almost every other shibboleth of the British right. At the height of the foot and mouth scare his conversion to vegetarianism was announced to the *Daily Telegraph* with the reflection that 'I still feel I'm missing out because the best meat I've ever had was at John Humphrys' house – he gets paid so much that he can afford an amazing piece of organic beef.' Humphrys regarded the vegetarianism 'with a large degree of scepticism. He loves feasting off the blood of new, young producers. And you couldn't say Rod was from the soft, liberal underbelly of the nation.'

Part of it is a game. Liddle came from outside the establishment. In his early twenties he studied at the London School of Economics, having already served an apprenticeship as a newspaper reporter. As an undergraduate he also worked full time for Barry Jones MP, then the Shadow Secretary of State for Wales, and proved his Stakhanovite work ethic by getting an excellent degree while earning a full-time salary. (Colleagues used to joke that Barry Jones did not know what he thought about any area of policy until Rod had told him.) I worked alongside him in the Shadow Cabinet corridor between 1985 and 1987, where he achieved what he has since accomplished at the BBC by managing to remain popular with left and right, with Roy Hattersley and Michael Meacher. He sometimes claimed to have invented Labour Party policy when he did not have the time to locate the official version. His personal peculiarities marked him out: a distrust of credit cards – even cheque guarantee cards – led him to extract all funds from the Co-op Bank in cash. Any extravagance was reserved for clothes and nightclubs, and Liddle amused more serious political activists by turning up at the House of Commons in generously cut silk shirts and the remains of the previous night's make-up.

But Liddle's private generosity routinely contradicts his swashbuckling, laid-back image, and he is clever and diligent enough never to appear ridiculous, as would a less able man who behaved as he does. There is something distinctly Peter Pan-ish about a man who wants to appear young, radical and alternative while entering early middle age in a patently establishment job.

He has certainly changed *Today* since he took the helm in 1998. Retaining an independence of mind rare among senior BBC staff, his instinct above all is as a campaigning newspaper editor, implacable in his belief that editors exist to make trouble for powerful people and powerful institutions, whatever their ideological positions. Liddle's pitch for the job included a clear-sighted commitment to original journalism. 'Roger Mosey believed that stories emerged from interviews,' says Stephen Mitchell, the head of Radio News. 'Rod believes they come from reporters. *Today* now has about a dozen dedicated reporters with time to break stories. It has more money for exclusives. The programme is budgeted to do that.' Liddle is adamant that his is the right approach – and not just for editorial reasons. 'When we do this original journalism, one of the reasons [is] it's cost effective. You've got a wonderful, cracking story. You run with it a six o'clock, six-thirty, seven – and it's in the news bulletins. It spreads throughout the programme.'

One of the biggest controversies under his editorship to date has been Andrew Gilligan's provocative story about a constitution for the EU. *Today* reported that a document was being drawn up for the EU, which some would see as the basis for a constitution for a federal European state. One of Sue MacGregor's cues, Liddle admits, 'said something like, "It's a federal Europe, it's a federal Europe."' The EU complained to the BBC, as apparently it does more than anyone else. Downing Street had condemned the report as a 'Euro scare-story' and labelled Andrew Gilligan, potentially libellously, as 'Gullible Gilligan'.

But calls to tame *Today* were also emanating from within the BBC. 'From time to time,' wrote Matt Wells, the *Guardian*'s media correspondent, in an article entitled 'Tame the Rottweilers' on Monday, 11 December 2000, 'something comes up that really raises the hackles of *Today*'s detractors, and lands the programme in trouble. And every time *Today* is in trouble, it is not just a bowl of hot water, but a great swirl of molten lava.' Wells reported that a senior journalist on another Radio Four programme believed the report had gone too far, that it threatened to undermine the BBC's reputation for impartiality and 'it was damaging to the BBC brand. What makes people annoyed,' added this courageously anonymous source, 'is that Rod thinks his job is to stir things up, and to hell with everyone else.' 'I think there is a feeling around the place,' said another BBC journalist, 'that some of them push things a bit too far in an effort to make something sound new.' A battle for the soul of the *Today* programme was raging within the BBC, argued Wells, between what he described as the 'Pathe News tendency' (who stand by the Corporation's traditional journalism of record) and the Liddle faction, which believes that *Today* has to be more ambitious if it is to maintain its place in the national consciousness. It is hardly surprising that the latter provokes controversy at the BBC.

Another piece of original journalism that caused trouble was Andrew Hosken's report, on the basis of an original survey, that Christmas 2000 would see a crisis in the NHS. 'Alastair [Campbell] rubbished it big-time at his briefing,' says Rod Liddle, 'and our bosses said, "Oh. Did we go too far?" Three days later Blair himself said there would be a crisis in the NHS, almost using exactly the same words. That's why, pinned up to my office door, there are "Fancy that!" press cuttings.' He acknowledges that such complaints were potentially damaging to the credibility of the *Today* programme, but says the danger lies not in the controversial journalism but in the BBC's plodding failure to defend itself immediately and aggressively. 'At eleven o'clock in the morning Alastair Campbell complains to the lobby. Then government ministers rubbish [the story] on the one o'clock news. You have to get your rebuttal out bloody quickly. The BBC is terrified of the press – absolutely terrified.' Challenged to admit that, while this may be the way complaints are dealt with by newspapers, it is not the BBC way, Liddle smiles and points at himself with his right index finger: 'Journalist!'

Liddle is resentful that the internal support available for a BBC editor breaking controversial news and irritating powerful interests is substantially less robust than it would be for a newspaper editor. In language rarely used by BBC staff, he accuses it of being 'run like the civil service – which means you don't do anything, you certainly don't promote your product. I mean, if I suggested going on television to talk, I would be refused. And the idea of taking responsibility for your programme, your product, is totally absent. You will always refer up. If you don't do a good job, they will always promote you into some fatuous middle-level bureaucratic job. Awful. Awful. I'm sure Greg Dyke will change it.'

Rod Liddle is quick to accept that he changed the programme because he had to. Political interviews had become harder to obtain. *Today* was no longer the only possible forum for important news and debate. But he is not convinced that *Today* has yet found the new style of political interviewing required to get the best out of a new generation of media-savvy politicians. Gordon Brown, the Chancellor of the Exchequer and a regular contributor to *Today*, 'has honed down his appearances on the *Today* programme to a degree that he will sometimes say nothing whatsoever in a thirty-minute interview,' according to Liddle. 'It is an astonishing feat. I mean, it's the sort of thing Radio Four makes games shows of.'

The result has been another change in *Today*, a return to the past implemented not because politicians are no longer available but because they are not always interesting. The programme has rediscovered its appetite for fun. 'Since 1997, politics has gone off the boil,' says Sue MacGregor, 'Rod has deliberately gone out to be a little naughty, perhaps attracting a younger audience, certainly getting a lot of attention in the papers.' The trenchant views expressed by Will Self and Freddie Forsyth in the 'Saturday Essay' slot provoke massive audience response. *Today*'s enthusiastic embrace of internet technology has been a spectacular success, with the programme's dedicated website attracting thousands, occasionally hundreds of thousands, of visitors every week.

One of Will Self's essays, however, occasioned rather more fun and games than anticipated. Rod Liddle got a call at home from the duty editor, who thought certain phrases of Self's were somewhat tasteless and might offend listeners. Having listened to the words in question, the editor agreed. He was all in favour of Will Self being controversial. He had no qualms about broadcasting a 'Saturday Essay' which suggested that Comic Relief is more concerned with massaging the consciences of the affluent than doing any real good. But some of Self's language was a bit pungent for a Saturday morning. Not the ideal accompaniment to coffee and croissants. The decision was easy. The essay could be edited without changing the meaning and, though the process eventually involved too many nervous phone calls and too much anxious contemplation, listeners would hear the sanitized version and never know what had been removed.

Imagine Liddle's surprise at 8.55 the next morning at hearing the inimitable tones of Will Self declaring that Britain's favourite charity extravaganza was 'all mutual masturbation and tit-beating'. That was the bit that was supposed to have come out.

It was not the first time, and it will not be the last. The digital recording of Self's essay had been edited precisely as agreed, but nobody had bothered to destroy the original and that was what ended up being broadcast. Liddle braced himself for a barrage of protests from 'outraged of Tunbridge Wells' who had almost certainly been listening to *Today* in the company of her brood of deeply impressionable children. He began to draft the letter of apology in his head.

There was not a single complaint. If listeners heard the comments – and at 8.55 on a Saturday morning there would have been considerably more than a million of them – they were either unshocked or amused. Probably the latter.

The truth is that *Today* in 2001 is more important than it has ever been. Multi-channel television has fragmented viewing habits. The nation no longer sits down together to watch the network television bulletins on the BBC or ITN. Conversations on buses and trains no longer revolve around the issues covered in them. It is truly breathtaking how many of the television executives who scream denials every time allegations of dumbing-down are made, privately acknowledge that this is precisely what has happened. They may call the process 'enhancing accessibility' or 'achieving relevance' but they know that what they mean is that television, in a doomed battle for ratings, now aims at the lowest common denominator.

This has been *Today*'s biggest asset. As television has become deliberately unintelligent, terrified to take risks and utterly lacking in courage and ambition, *Today* has done the opposite. By remaining what Edward Stourton calls 'ruthlessly ambitious in its pursuit of intelligent journalism', it has proved that Britain still has an appetite for a national conversation. 'The rolling news format is something you can get everywhere. ITN, Sky, BBC News 24. They are different but in the end they are all doing the same job, whereas something like *Today* is doing a very distinctive job. It's not something you could sit down and design on the back of an envelope. It's a sort of organic thing. When people say, "What is the BBC?" you can point to it and they know what you mean.'

To the extent that this modern prominence has been achieved against a background of great uncertainty and caution in BBC News and Current Affairs, it is a tribute to the talent and ingenuity of the programme editor. As one senior BBC executive told me, 'When the *Telegraph* attacked Rod Liddle for becoming a veggie, it also said his programme was excellent. If the tribune of Conservatism, the newspaper most loved by those who used to say it was a socialist conspiracy, now thinks *Today* is excellent then it really is surpassing expectations.'

As the general election of 7 June 2001 loomed, the extent of *Today*'s recovery from the doldrums was again illustrated by the obsessive interest of politicians and those who do their bidding. In April Alastair Campbell, having given up any hope of rendering *Today* irrelevant, had returned to the tried and tested practice of bullying the programme, urging its editor to avoid focusing on scandals involving government figures and accusing *Today* of 'following the agenda' of hostile newspapers like the *Daily Mail*. This pre-emptive strike reflected above all Downing Street's concern about *Today*'s relentless pursuit of the Europe Minister

Keith Vaz, whose reputation had been dented by his refusal to fully co-operate with a Parliamentary inquiry into allegations of misconduct.

Today ignored this rather clumsy attempt to dictate the programme's agenda before the election campaign had even started. A programme spokesman (Liddle unaccustomedly operating under a thin cloak of anonymity) insouciantly predicted that 'I am expecting a letter every two or three days once the election starts.'

The campaign began well, with Jim Naughtie, Edward Stourton and Sue MacGregor taking the *Today* 'battle bus' on tour around the country, and John Humphrys presenting five days a week from Television Centre. In his *Guardian* column Rod Liddle recorded a moment of surreal humour when a slug dropped out of Stourton's hair onto his dinner plate during a pre-programme meal in Taunton.

Early success came when Humphrys subjected the Prime Minister to an entertaining and very 'off message' interrogation about sleaze. It was precisely what Alastair Campbell had asked *Today* not to do and, when Humphrys asked Blair to reveal whether he would offer 'absolute confidence, trust and support' for Mr Vaz, the Prime Minister, sounding irritable, displayed a distinctly selective memory with regard to the findings of the Parliamentary Commissioner for Standards, Elizabeth Filkin. A senior ministerial colleague, meanwhile, had warned that 'it is up to the major parties to set the agenda, not the BBC'. Humphrys' interview with the Prime Minister lasted for twenty-one minutes, a marathon grilling by *Today* standards. Ten of them were dedicated to the topic of sleaze. Campbell's bullying had backfired.

It was proof that *Today* had no intention of accepting New Labour's definition of editorial responsibility. So there was internal anger about a BBC management dictat, circulated by Stephen Mitchell on the same morning as the Blair interview, which appeared to endorse elements of the government's approach. It instructed journalists not to make further direct approaches to Keith Vaz, which *Today* reporters had been assiduously trying to do, many staff at the programme fearing their bosses were being too credulous and sympathetic to claims that the minister was seriously ill.

Right of centre columnists, notably Steven Glover in the *Daily Mail*, concluded that the memo reflected a mood of overt sycophancy towards a Labour Party set fair for a second convincing election victory. Those suspicions looked to have been partially confirmed when evidence emerged that Vaz had been campaigning in his constituency while insisting he was too unwell to respond to reporters' questions.

But *Today* did not back off and eventually relentless pursuit paid dividends. Reporter Barney Choudhury did eventually manage to stick his microphone in front of Mr Vaz. Listeners were treated to one of the most eccentric interviews in recent memory. Choudhury asked Vaz about his health, the allegations of impropriety and his suitability for office. Vaz adopted the broken record technique and spoke about his visit to a cancer care facility in his constituency. It did not matter what question the reporter asked, the minister refused to be diverted. If the interrogation revealed anything, it emerged from what Vaz did not say.

A fortnight later on 5 June 2001, a mere two days before polling day, *Today* resumed its pursuit of the hapless Vaz. Investigative work by reporter Andrew Hosken discovered Land Registry documents which appeared to prove that the Europe Minister had, when challenged by the parliamentary inquiry, failed to declare all of his property portfolio. To Labour campaign managers it looked like a vendetta. But Hosken's research was too meticulous for that allegation to stick. The revelations were particularly galling for the Labour leadership because they were broadcast less than twelve hours after the Prime Minister had mounted an aggressive defence of Vaz's integrity in an interview with Jeremy Paxman on the previous evening's *Newsnight* programme.

The Vaz episode was a good illustration of *Today*'s new editorial philosophy. Coverage of previous general election campaigns had been planned with meticulous attention to detail, leaving little room for spontaneous journalism and too few opportunities to respond to breaking stories. In 2001 Liddle and his team abandoned the comfort-blanket of planned coverage and took a three-pronged approach.

They planned a few major interviews with party leaders and

other senior figures, refused to follow the agendas set by party press conferences and deliberately set out to uncover stories and opinions other broadcasters would ignore. So, on Friday, 25 May the controversial Harrods owner Mohammed al Fayed shared his distinctly unconventional views on British politics. Days later *Today* lined up an interview with health secretary Alan Millburn by interviewing the father of Jennifer Russell, the little girl at the centre of the 'Jennifer's ear' fiasco – a row over a Labour party political broadcast on NHS waiting lists that had derailed its 1992 election campaign. The Jennifer's ear idea worked well. The same could not be said of the Fayed experiment.

Still, it was good anti-establishment stuff cheekily designed to challenge New Labour and embarrass the ascendant party during one of the most predictable re-election campaigns in British electoral history. This transparent desire to get up Labour's nose was confirmed by investigations into foot and mouth disease, asylum seekers in the Prime Minister's Sedgefield constituency and intensive efforts to uncover the potential for inefficiency and even fraud in the new system for registering postal votes. The latter involved *Today* reporter Andrew Gilligan registering numerous postal votes in the names of dead citizens in a key marginal constituency.

Perhaps inevitably, *Today*'s desire to set its own agenda, confronting issues the Labour campaign team did not want discussed, provoked retaliation. On Friday, 1 June, John Humphrys made an unusual apology to listeners. For the first time in three weeks of active campaigning no senior Labour politician had appeared on the show. 'The Labour Party has failed to put up any government spokesman on any issues,' said Humphrys, 'although we did ask for an interview with Chris Smith or Claire Short yesterday morning. At least one of them had not been told of the request by midnight last night, so our apologies for that.'

The minister who did not know of the programme's interest was the culture secretary Chris Smith. *Today* sources concluded that government spin doctors were reluctant to allow Smith to answer questions about the possibility of spending national lottery proceeds to subsidize Labour's planned investment in schools and the health service. Though Claire Short's non-appearance was not explained, BBC staff guessed that Ms Short was considered a liability by the party leadership, with her reputation for what New Labour calls 'going off-message' and what ordinary citizens might call speaking her mind. She had done it on day one of the campaign, lending her voice to the sceptical reception of the Prime Minister's election announcement at a London school, when he appeared before an audience of adolescent girls against the backdrop of a stained-glass window. Humphrys' on-air apology was broadcast after the programme had offered to accept any Labour frontbencher the party cared to put up, and a final appeal to Millbank Tower made at 8.07 on the Friday morning.

The snub to *Today* was an illustration of just how carefully stage-managed Labour's campaign was and how irritating Millbank Tower found the programme's refusal to play by their rules. Labour spin doctors aroused amused contempt at Television Centre by telling *Today* staff that any listeners who wanted to hear from government ministers could listen to direct broadcasts of party press conferences via the internet. The *Daily Telegraph*'s Matt Born reported that Labour was 'wary of suffering any further embarrassments at the hands of [John] Humphrys'. Besides mauling the Prime Minister on the subject of sleaze, by that stage *Today*'s interrogator-in-chief had done a still more devastating job on the health minister Yvette Cooper in an interview about the funding of cancer care hospices. Cooper had only herself to blame. She should have been briefed about Humphrys particular interest in hospice care. The presenter had been at his wife's bedside when she died in one.

It has rarely been New Labour style to accept blame when ministers flounder under questioning. The Millbank response is usually to blame the messenger. 'We were just following our own agenda and trying to pursue original journalism,' says Rod Liddle. 'The Liberal Democrats and the Tories will go along with that. Labour won't.'

For *Today* it was the most bruising encounter of the campaign. But problems arose from less predictable sources too. It was Liddle's investigative approach that came closest to going seriously wrong. The story was not election-inspired, but it broke midway through the campaign. In spring 2001 BBC social affairs correspondent Barney Choudhury had travelled to

Oldham for *Today* to investigate allegations of serious racial tension. A group of teenage Asian Muslims told him that militants were creating racially segregated areas in the town. His report, broadcast in April, included their claim that Oldham now contained no-go areas in which white residents were not welcome.

Three days after the report was broadcast, Oldham resident Walter Chamberlain, a seventy-six-year-old veteran of World War II, was attacked and brutally beaten. Police charged a fifteen-year-old Asian boy with racially motivated grievous bodily harm. Mr Chamberlain did not claim that the youths who attacked him shouted racist slogans. His adult children said they did not want the assault treated as a racist incident and were explicit in their insistence that they did not think it was one. But tempers were becoming frayed. The local newspaper ran a front page story in which the probably apocryphal quote 'get out of our area' ran alongside a picture of Walter Chamberlain's badly injured face.

For extreme-right political groups the suggestion that a war veteran had been the victim of Asian violence in a British town was manna from heaven. The openly racist British National Party seized on the innocent Mr Chamberlain as a propaganda tool. BNP activists circulated posters of his injuries in a campaign to foment hatred between whites and Asians. In Oldham, community leaders muttered that a problem which had been confined to tiny groups of disenchanted adolescents until the *Today* report gave it a national profile was suddenly being exploited by dedicated racists keen for their own poisonous ends.

At first Oldham's troubles seemed to have been submerged by the bigger issues of the general election campaign. Then, on the evening of Saturday, 26 May 2001, the town erupted. A brief altercation outside a chip shop between one white youth and one Asian provoked riots involving hundreds of people. Police vehicles were burned, shops smashed and looted, and the local newspaper firebombed. In Oldham and beyond, voices began to ask a blunt question: was the *Today* programme responsible for provoking the Oldham riots?

The anodyne answer is straightforward. No reporter or editor can be held responsible if criminals conclude that a provocative allegation justifies the throwing of petrol bombs. But that is too glib. There is anecdotal evidence that the *Today* report encouraged the BNP to focus on Oldham. Locals argue that racist propaganda and incitement reached unprecedented heights in the weeks after *Today* gave the no-go allegation an audience of millions.

BBC managers say that if any national newspaper had heard claims that some black youths were trying to set up no-go areas in Oldham, 'most of them would have run it in a much more inflammatory way than *Today* did'. 'What you cannot deny,' one told me, 'is that there is a lot of anger in Oldham among Pakistani youths and that there is antagonism towards both the police and the local white population for various historic reasons. I don't see that reporting that and reporting the fact that some of them have decided to take the law into their own hands is inciting a riot.'

But that is a non-denial. A senior *Today* journalist told me that the 'problem of stirring up trouble did occur to us', and explained that 'if you do journalism which is a little bit risky – and that was a bit risky – then you can run into problems. In the past *Today* did not do that sort of thing. Now we do.'

There are significant problems with this strategy. *Today* is not a newspaper. It has none of the ideological affiliations that make British newspapers less than scrupulously objective. It is a BBC programme, funded by the licence fee and constrained by commitments to truth and impartiality. This should not make the programme risk averse – such an attitude has rendered too much BBC news and current affairs output bland and unchallenging. But it does place it under an onerous burden of responsibility.

Infuriating politicians is a low risk activity. They are more than able to look after themselves, and the electorate regards many of them with naked contempt. Playing with racial intolerance is a qualitatively different matter, risking not just stiff letters of protest from Alastair Campbell or Amanda Platell, but real anger and violence. Quite simply, the BBC is badly organized to cope with issues like the Oldham riots. As Rod Liddle contends, it treats political complaints with a seriousness they simply do not deserve, but sometimes seems strangely untroubled by issues that impact on real lives.

Investigative journalism has to be carefully policed. It is often based on hunches and must be ruthlessly tested less the reporter falls into the trap of giving too much weight to assertions which support his original reason for taking an interest in an issue. Mature reflection on *Today*'s Oldham report might conclude that it lent excessive credence to a barely credible assertion. Barney Choudhury's report contained too little detail to substantiate the claim about no-go areas. *Today*'s remoteness from the community it was investigating encouraged it to make assertions that had not been extensively reported locally. This does not make them untrue – journalists know that those who participate in or are affected by local disputes are least likely to tell the truth about them. Distance, on the other hand, can lend courage and objectivity – but it demands scepticism too.

Today in 2001 was an exciting place to work. Reporters were being encouraged to chase ideas and check hunches. Many of the results did justice to Rod Liddle's faith in troublemaking investigative journalism. There was a sense that a relatively new team was breaking new ground on *Today*. But it has not re-invented radio journalism – some of the reporting commissioned by one of Liddle's predecessors, Phil Harding, was equally agenda-setting. *Today* has just applied good editorial instincts with new passion and drive. I still think *Today* needs to be careful, not cautious, if it is to combine the best of the new with a reputation that has been built up over decades. As for Rod Liddle, perhaps Greg Dyke should clone him and ensure his ideas are applied to a much wider range of BBC news programmes.

Whether the Director General follows that advice or not, Rod Liddle's successor at *Today* will have a tough act to follow. He must continue the stubborn investigation of a government, which, like the Conservatives in the early 1990s, has already passed the peak of its popularity. That will exacerbate tension between the programme team and BBC management. It might be easier to compromise than to risk the wrath of a board of governors with too obvious Blairite sympathies.

But compromise would be a disaster. *Today* attracts listeners and demands respect because it is so obviously not part of the bland, neutered morass of news programming intelligent Britons race to turn off. *Today* must continue to challenge listeners, politicians and BBC managers alike. It must keep the dissident mentality that has made it such an excellent servant of democracy.

Other dilemmas must be faced as well. *Today* has been too slow to understand the changing shape of Britain. Though it serves every part of Britain better than any local or regional BBC news service, it does not serve Scotland, Wales or Northern Ireland as effectively as it serves London and the Home Counties. That failure is all the more stark because the regional alternatives the BBC provides to scrutinize devolved Britain conspicuously fail to do the job. *Today* must learn to understand the new Britain and to interrogate those who govern it as ferociously as it does their masters in Whitehall and Westminster.

While dealing with this political and regional agenda, a new editor must also make key decisions about his presenters. The present line-up is too fluid and confusing. A choice must be made between Allan Little and Ed Stourton. Sue MacGregor's replacement must be named.

And all this must be achieved against a background of hesitancy and some hostility within the BBC. *Today* is not a new idea. It is sophisticated, diverse and sometimes uncomfortable. *Today* creates problems as good journalism is supposed to. It offends the powerful and scares the cautious. *Today* could easily be starved of resources and intellectually eviscerated. If the BBC chooses to spend too heavily on failed experiments in minority-interest broadcasting, that is what will happen. Twenty-four hour digital television news is obviously modern, but it is hard to identify any criteria upon which it can be called popular. *Today*'s strength at the beginning of the twenty-first century is that it is almost impossible to identify criteria upon which it can be called anything else.

Acknowledgements

This book is not remotely official, but writing it was made a lot easier by the generous help of many friends at the BBC. I can not identify them all, and some will prefer it that way, but special thanks are due to Stephen Mitchell and Rod Liddle. I would also like to recognize Phil Harding for recruiting me to *Today* in the first place, Viorel Buligan for guiding me through Timisoara and Walid abu Zeid for teaching me to recognize the difference between French and Iraqi military vehicles before the issue became critical.

Saturday afternoons would not have been as sweet without Partick Thistle Football Club who diverted me when I needed a lift and won the Scottish Second Division Championship in the process. Truly there is only one team in the Bible.

The sound track was provided by Janis Joplin, Bob Dylan and Steely Dan. Graham Coster of Aurum Press was calm, wise and benign. To him my thanks for commissioning me in the first place and for numerous improvements to the script.

The views expressed are my own. So are the mistakes.